THE PASTORAL MASQUERADE
DISGUISE AND IDENTITY IN *L'ASTRÉE*

STANFORD FRENCH AND ITALIAN STUDIES

executive editor
JEAN-MARIE APOSTOLIDÈS

editor
MARC BERTRAND

editorial board
BRIGITTE CAZELLES
ROBERT GREER COHN
JEAN-PIERRE DUPUY
JOHN FRECCERO
RENÉ GIRARD
HANS ULRICH GUMBRECHT
ROBERT HARRISON
RALPH HESTER
ODILE HULLOT-KENTOR
PAULINE NEWMAN-GORDON
JEFFREY SCHNAPP
MICHEL SERRES
CAROLYN SPRINGER
JAMES WINCHELL

managing editor
KATARINA KIVEL

founder
ALPHONSE JUILLAND

volume LXXIII

DEPARTMENT OF FRENCH AND ITALIAN
STANFORD UNIVERSITY

THE PASTORAL MASQUERADE
DISGUISE AND IDENTITY IN *L'ASTRÉE*

LAURENCE A. GREGORIO

1992

ANMA LIBRI

Stanford French and Italian Studies is a collection of scholarly publications devoted to the study of French and Italian literature and language, culture and civilization. Occasionally it will allow itself excursions into related Romance areas.

Stanford French and Italian Studies will publish books, monographs, and collections of articles centering around a common theme, and is open to scholars associated with academic institutions other than Stanford.

The collection is published by the Department of French and Italian, Stanford University and ANMA Libri.

© 1992 by ANMA Libri & Co., P.O. Box 876, Saratoga, Calif. 95071
and Department of French and Italian, Stanford University
All rights reserved
LC 91-77568
ISBN 0-915838-89-3
Printed in the United States of America

Acknowledgements

I would like to express my greatest thanks to Professor Jean V. Alter of the University of Pennsylvania for his generous and invaluable advice concerning my work over the years. I offer my expression of gratitude to my colleagues Professors Robert Viti, C. Kerr Thompson, Charles Zabrowski, Leslie Cahoon and Alain Faucon at Gettysburg College whose help and suggestions made this project easier for me. My thanks also go to the administration of Gettysburg College and the College's Paul H. Rhoads Teaching and Professional Development Fund for material aid in the research and publication of this book. Finally, I wish to recognize the support of my family upon which I relied constantly during my work.

L.A.G.

To my wife, Marcia,
and our children, Joseph, Julie and Elena

Table of Contents

Introduction	1
1. Tradition of Disguise	3
2. An Overview of Disguise in *L'Astrée*	17
3. *Travestissement*	29
4. The Other Physical Disguises	44
5. Behavioral Disguises	56
6. General Inferences on Disguise	63
7. The Markers of Identity	73
8. Characters and Their Markers	94
Conclusion: The Society in Disguise	112
Appendix	124
Bibliography	132

Introduction

The work that follows is intended, in some measure, to be a poetics of disguise and character-identification in the French pastoral romance, taking the masterwork of Honoré d'Urfé as the capstone of the pastoral tradition in France. Its objective is to make plain both the ways in which identity may be masked, and the ways in which identity is crafted for recognition by the textual society. Part of its inspiration comes from the fine work of John D. Lyons which elucidates the dynamics of the mask in the French baroque theater.

While consideration for the tradition of the pastoral narrative prior to the seventeenth century will provide our point of departure, the greater part of our concentration will be on *L'Astrée*. The edition to which we refer will be that edited by H. Vaganay in 5 volumes (Lyon: Masson, 1925-1928). References will appear parenthetically by volume (Roman numeral) and page (Arabic numeral) in the course of the study. Our attention will be directed to that part of the work which is conventionally attributed to the pen of d'Urfé himself, that is, the first four volumes, the last of which was, by some accounts, in the latter stages of drafting at his death in 1625.

The work of Eglal Henein most recent to this writing raises interesting questions regarding the conventional acceptance of the fourth volume (understood to have been completed by d'Urfé's secretary, Baro, and published in 1628) as a reliable and definitive continuation of d'Urfé's own work.[1] Professor Henein admits that these doubts cannot be resolved because of the imperfection of the historical record

---

[1] Eglal Henein, "Les Vicissitudes de la quatrième partie de *L'Astrée*," *Revue d'Histoire Littéraire de la France* 6 (1990) 883-898.

in the establishment of the text of *L'Astrée*; nonetheless she cites stylistic and thematic divergences in the fourth volume that set it apart from the first three, differences which might cause one to wonder how much of the work is d'Urfé's, and how much Baro's, if harmony and consistency are to be presupposed in the text. These concerns notwithstanding, the present study will accept the fourth volume of Baro, on the strength of critical tradition (since doubts have yet to be substantiated with historical evidence) and in light of what is known about Baro and his association with d'Urfé; for the rest, many of the thematic divergences that develop over the course of the text (see Eglal Henein, 887-894) will figure in a pattern of development in *L'Astrée* which, it is hoped, will seem logical and compelling to the reader of this study.

It would be best for us to make clear at this point our understanding of certain terms that will be recurring. "Pastoral ethic" will be used to denote what the textual society observes as general morality (honesty, regard for law, etc.), combined with a great respect for both religion and the social hierarchy; along with these is included the commitment to platonic principles of love. We shall also use the term "heroic code" to signify a mixture of chivalrous values (courage, loyalty, dedication to the good cause, etc.) with many of the values glorified in the bucolic tradition (tranquility, simplicity, love of Nature, and so on). Finally, the term "identity" will be used to refer not only to the name of a character, but to the composite of markers by which that character is recognized: not only *who* the character is, but *what* he or she represents.

To facilitate the reading of this study, there appears in the appendix an annotated list of the considerable cast of characters in *L'Astrée*. All named characters, along with the most important of those known by epithet only, are indexed there in alphabetical order. Each entry is accompanied by information and page references which situate the character in the text's great flow of events.

Let us turn first to the motif of disguise, as it figures in the tradition of the pastoral romance and in the literature of France prior to d'Urfé, and as it works its great influence on the thematic and narrative strategies of *L'Astrée*. Then, having studied the ways in which identity is hidden, we shall consider the processes by which identity is assembled for recognition by characters and reader alike.

1. Tradition of Disguise

Certain aspects of *L'Astrée*, thematic wellspring of inspiration for much of its century's fiction, have captured the minds of its readers and critics since the days of its first appearance. None more so than the topic of love, the interest which brought a first popular readership to the romance. Nothing could come as less of a surprise with a text that devotes so much of its considerable volume not only to labyrinthine intrigues of the heart, but also to a lengthy casuistry of love. Love's nuances, its rhetoric and subtle workings have assumed marked priority in the attention of the text's students, and certainly not without justification since love is far and away the preponderant motif of action and discourse.[1]

In a sense, the study undertaken here departs from critical tradition since it is not primarily concerned with the love motif, even though no consideration of any pastoral romance can, at any point, stray far from that subject. We turn instead to the study of the phenomena of disguise and identity within the text, but we are nonetheless mindful of the fact that the motif of love remains close to the center of our discussion. Whatever they do — shepherds and nobles, good and villainous alike — the characters do for love, for the most part. If they disguise themselves, it is often with amorous intent; if identity is called into question, it is usually with thematic ramifications in a love relationship. Therefore, to discuss disguise and identity is also to discuss

---

[1] Love is given lengthy consideration by Henri Bochet, "*L'Astrée*: ses origines, son importance dans la formation de la littérature classique," diss., Geneva, 1923. See also Maurice Magendie, L'Astrée: *analyse et extraits* (Paris: Perrin, 1928) for a study of this topic. The work of Jacques Ehrmann, *Un Paradis désespéré: l'amour et l'illusion*

love. But our attention will fall primarily on the mask and the identity that underlies it, with a goal of pointing up their places of prominence in the organization of the text.

This is not to imply that the fertile topic of the mask has up until now escaped the attention of critical study. The fine article of Jean D. Charron, for example, treats the Celadon/Alexis disguise, but it could not be expected to exhaust the subject; likewise, the collaborative work of Andrea Cali and Carmela Ferrandes shows fine sensitivity to the social dynamics behind the motif of the mask, and it raises the right issues about the motif's underlying thematic forces, even if its scope is limited to the first three of Celadon's disguises.[2] For the rest, it could be said of other work on *L'Astrée* that the mask has aroused tangential interest (most notably in the excellent work of Jacques Ehrmann[3]), but the subject remains to be studied in depth.

The fact that the motif of the mask is not new to narrative prose at the beginning of the seventeenth century (or to the immediate precursors of *L'Astrée* in the pastoral tradition, for that matter) directs our attention to its role in earlier literature — a corpus of works with which d'Urfé was certainly familiar, and which were, in all probability, formative in the pastoral tradition. We need not even dwell long with the evident dynamism of mask in early theater for the point to become abundantly clear, for in prose and narrative poetry alone the mask is visible and vital far into the past.

In theater, of course, disguise is an inviting topic to approach. By its nature, theater is predicated on the disguises actors bring to life, but in addition to this, there is a rich and ancient tradition of physical, visible play on the mask. Critical explanations for the physical masking of all actors in classical Greek theater have been proffered ranging from the pragmatic (for purposes of audience recognition and voice amplification) to the mytho/anthropological (to protect the players from malevolent forces) to the esthetic (to enhance the effect of

---

dans L'Astrée (New Haven: Yale University Press; Paris: Presses Universitaires de France, 1963) is quite thorough and probably the best treatment of the subject. See also Michel Zéraffa, "Raisons du coeur et raison de *L'Astrée*," in *Le Récit amoureux*, ed. and foreword, Didier Coste, ed. Michel Zéraffa (Paris: Champ Vallon, 1984) 39-52.

[2] Jean D. Charron, "Le Thème de la 'Métamorphose' dans *L'Astrée*," *XVIIe Siècle* 101 (4e trimestre 1973) 3-13. Andrea Cali and Carmela Ferrandes, "L'infrazione al codice: il 'déguisement' nell'*Astrée* di Honoré d'Urfé," in *Il Romanzo al tempo di Luigi XIII* (Bari: Adriatica; Paris: Nizet, 1976) 13-38.

[3] Ehrmann 72-86.

the role). Strong cases can be made for all these, but the point is that, even in its earliest forms, theater began to contribute strongly to a motif that made identity a problematic matter, one that could be exploited for dramatic effect beyond the obvious physical implications.

It can be argued reasonably that the potent motif of the mask in theater was itself sufficient to plant the thematic seeds of disguise for all of literature. It need not become an issue of debate here. But the fact is that, even without recourse to the dramatic tradition, one can point to an ancient *topos* which enables the reader of later pastoral literature to make better sense of complicated play in identity.

In the very early texts in the genres of lyric and narrative as well, the issues of disguise, recognition and character identity are crucial items of interest in plot, thematic outlay, and character development; in a phrase, they are ubiquitous and vital. The *Odyssey* is, of course, replete with masking. In the *Aeneid*, disguise is a powerful tool in the hands of the gods, as with Venus (in book I) who appears to Aeneas in the costume of Diana[4]; repeatedly in the last six books, Juno sends disguised mortals to do her bidding.

But it is in the area of the ancient prose romances where the motif of disguise and the thematics of identity show a most prodigious development and bear the strongest resemblance to what they are destined to become in the romances of a much later century. Greek romances dating from the second or third centuries A.D. bear witness to a fully developed literary tradition of disguise and crises of identity across barriers of social class, not to mention climactic scenes of anagnorisis where identities are finally established. Let us consider, for example, Longus' *Daphnis and Chloe* which scholars place prior to the fifth century A.D.[5] Thematic resemblances with d'Urfé's masterwork abound (and of course come as no surprise, given d'Urfé's erudition and thorough grounding in the classics). Here we see a tale of two babies found and supposed to be of noble stock, raised as shepherds in a society of virtuous, dutiful shepherds, where characters are wholly beholden to love, and where characters tell inserted narratives; it is set in a society which reveres its Nymphs, where temples full of significant paintings become important to the narrative, and there is even a red-haired shepherd who (much in the manner

---

[4] See Virgil, *Aeneid*, ed. T.E. Page, 2 vols. (London: Macmillan, 1960) 1: 10, lines 318 ff.

[5] This work may be found in *Three Greek Romances*, tr. Moses Hadas (Indianapolis, New York, Kansas City: Bobbs-Merrill, 1964).

of *L'Astrée*'s Hylas) is overly assertive in matters of love. Thus, thoroughly integrated with the stock thematic stuff of the pastoral tradition, with the peripeties of action and the thematics of a rationalized kind of love, the motif of hidden identity plays a central role.

It is no wonder that the mask enjoys such a rich and ancient tradition in prose. It gives rise like no other motif to structural irony, complication of action, heightening of tension, and even humorous effect. So no one could be surprised to encounter it and its attendant crises of identity in text after text through the ages, from the ancients up to the baroque and beyond.

The literature of the Middle Ages in particular exploits the phenomenon of disguise — this in spite of the commonly accepted generalities concerning the era, those of "medieval fixity," humorless clerical control of cultural activity, and "the pietistic note that dominated" those centuries.[6] While it is true that the Catholic church, as early as the fourth century, condemned masks and disguise as demonic and contrary to the truth, the literature that comes down to us from all subsequent centuries does not fail to participate fully in the tradition of the mask, inherited from its pagan ancestors. Nowhere is this more true than in the corpus of French literature, where *nouvelles*, epics, *romans*, *fabliaux*, and lyric poetry alike all put to great use the motif of disguise.

La Vie de Saint Alexis in the eleventh century makes much of the issues of disguise and the mask which changes identity across lines of social class. The protagonist, born to the highest nobility, rids himself of earthly possessions and lives among the poor; his greatest fear is thus expressed: "...molt fortment se redotet / de ses parenz, qued il nel reconoissent..."[7] Indeed he achieves sanctity by hiding his identity from his family under whose stairway he dwells in poverty for seventeen years.

In several of Tristan's permutations through the centuries does he employ the devices of disguise, appearing as a leper, a madman, a beggar or a minstrel. Merlin the magician, of course, makes repeated use of disguise to achieve his ends. The same holds for many of the great recurring characters of medieval legend, characters heroic or villainous, that disguise provides a ready and effective means to

---

[6] William A. Nitze and E. Preston Dargan, *A History of French Literature*, 3rd ed. (New York: Holt, 1938) 17.

[7] *La Vie de Saint Alexis* in *Chrestomathie de l'ancien français*, 12th ed., ed. Karl Bartsch (New York and London: Hafner, 1969) 20-21.

enhance one's efforts. Thus it is that Guillaume and Yvain find it expeditious to change their identities. Other heroic characters, like Perceval in *Le Conte du Graal* and the protagonist of *Le Bel Inconnu*, find themselves in a different crisis of identity where they remain unaware of their true names, and thus are in quest of themselves. In other words, the establishment of identity becomes the center of interest in cases where the heroic character is deprived of such a means of recognition.

Numerous nonhuman characters in medieval literature don masks with varying intentions. Satan is most often seen in a mask for temptation. Renart passes for a *jongleur*. *Faux semblant* is a character in the *Roman de la Rose*. Fauvel is the great trickster and master of disguise. And it is the *Roman de Fauvel* which calls our attention to the *charivari* of the fourteenth century, carnivalesque church-related festivals in which participants dressed up as devils and the like.

The motif of the mask in the Middle Ages is not by any means limited to the games characters play for amusement or love. Nor are the thematics of identity limited to the dramatic effect of the quest which they sometimes engender. *Les Cent Nouvelles Nouvelles*[8] is a collection of tales in which disguise and *travestissement* serve the purpose of flouting the priorities of social institutions.

So, even if we limit our attention to the sweep of French literature prior to the Renaissance (and fictional prose, at that), not mentioning other likely sources of influence like the Bible and the theatrical tradition, we see a very richly developed *topos* that is handed down to the literati of the fifteenth and sixteenth centuries. The unavoidable impression we get is that, in literature dating from antiquity and through the Middle Ages, disguises of all sorts, borne by characters of all sorts for all sorts of reasons, furnish a ready and highly effective means for circumventing inconveniences of identity recognition; clearly the stylized literary mask flies in the face of the *vraisemblable*, but its appearance is so ubiquitous and so generally accepted in the course of literature that it takes on the aspect of an institution in the fictive universe. From the earliest literary prose onward, family members will fail to recognize one another, members of one sex can pass for members of the other, supposedly intransigent barriers of social caste can be crossed, totally new identities can be forged, all with a change of clothing or some equally superficial physical alteration. The

---

[8] *Les Cent Nouvelles Nouvelles*, ed. F.P. Sweetser (Geneva and Paris: Droz, TLF, 1966).

motif is traditionally a powerful one indeed, able to produce remarkable effects and create havoc within a fictive society's identity system. That it should appear before us in the French baroque novel in full force, then, can be no source of wonder; it is the dynamics and the more subtle implications of the mask in the pastoral romance that will come to light as we proceed.

With all of its play on the mask and on systems of identification, the pastoral novel came to full fruition in the Renaissance. France did not inherit the genre directly from antiquity or from its own medieval literature; rather it is from Italy by way of Spain that interest in the pastoral prose tradition is kindled in France during the early years of the seventeenth century. The prototypical romance is the *Arcadia* of Jacobo Sannazaro (1458-1530), taken in great measure as a model by the Spanish popularizer of the pastoral romance, Jorge de Montemayor (1520?-1561, Portugese by birth but Castillian by choice) in his widely read and enormously influential *Diana* (1559). The pastoral flourished in Spain in the late sixteenth century under the pens of Gaspar Gil Polo (d. 1591) whose *Diana enamorada* (1564) goes hand-in-glove with the work of Montemayor and, notably, Cervantes (*La Galatea*, 1585) — notably, because it is in Cervantes' later masterwork, *Don Quijote* (1605-1615), that the romance genre comes under blistering attack. By the beginning years of the seventeenth century, the popularity of the pastoral in Spain was supplanted by interest in the picaresque, but there remained sufficient enthusiasm into the 1630s for Gonzalo de Saavedra's *Los pastores del Bétis* (1633) to be a success. As the pastoral's popularity in Spain and Italy was waning during those years, in France it was just coming into vogue with the publication of *L'Astrée* (1607-1628).

For our purposes, the point is that d'Urfé by absolutely no means was writing in a vacuum. The fact that he took Sannazaro and Montemayor as models is well documented in scholarship.[9] So is the fact that he read Spanish, Italian, and Greek voraciously, amassing what Antoine Adam calls his "vaste culture" (Adam 114). Thematics ranging from the platonic discussion of love to the motif of the mask are to be found in abundance in those authors that d'Urfé emulated. Therefore it is not our goal to attribute the great motif of the mask to *L'Astrée* as an innovation; instead, we propose to examine what the

---

[9] See Nitze and Dargan 229 and Antoine Adam, *Histoire de la littérature française au XVIIe siècle*, 5 vols. (Paris: Editions Domat Montchrestien, 1948) 1: 118-119.

motif has become in the hands of d'Urfé and what are its unique implications for the text's fictive society.

As far as a general theory of disguise in pastoral narrative is concerned, there are several areas of function and effect that are of interest to us. First is the most germane to literary study, the *textual* function of disguise. There is, of course, an aesthetic aspect to disguise in the pastoral, namely, that its obvious testing of verisimilitude, to the extreme is one means of underscoring the imaginitive, artistic nature of the text, and framing the reader's reception of the work in the context of artistic experience. Likewise, the appearance of such a stylized "mask" constitutes an observance of a longstanding tradition, a participation in ancient conventions of the genre that helps situate the text in a current of literary history. And for the purposes of narrative itself, the mask is a great tool for the advancement of action, for the heightening of tension, for the development of character, and so on.

A second element of the mask deserving mention is its *psychological* aspect. This significance cannot be overstated, as the mask is abundantly wealthy in interpretations pertinent to the text itself and its relation to the world. True, the mask serves as a tool for characters as they work out problems or as they approach crises of identity, and it facilitates role-playing with whatever psychological advantages that has to offer. But more importantly, the mask offers a couple of great dimensions to characterization which would otherwise be unavailable. On the one hand, it affords characters a means of bringing their fantasies to life, and hence to show the reader what lies beneath the surface of individual personalities. On the other hand, the mask is a device that permits the multiplication of one's persona, allowing for contradictory elements of personality to surface. A most obvious illustration of the latter in the pastoral is the ease with which characters don the guise of the opposite sex; indeed, rarely is this disguise solely a physical one, as characters tend usually to experience the nature, traits and perceptions unique to the gender to which they have "acceded" via the mask. In general, then, disguise furnishes the psychological plan of the narrative with a marketplace of identity exchange, where characters may make themselves open to experiences otherwise inaccessible to them.

A third perspective which may readily be taken on the mask in literature is the *anthropological*, that is to say, to study the mask as an element of ritual if its function in the text so warrants. In *L'Astrée*, the case can certainly be made that the mask serves in the society's rituals of entertainment, and especially in its habits of courtship. Where characters take immediate refuge in disguise to counter the rigors of the code of love, where identity becomes a medium of communication and courtship, there the mask takes on a social value greater than its mere ability to hide something; there it has taken on strength in society's ethical/ideological arena, especially in cases where it is recommended as a course of action by spiritual or philosophical authorities (for example, Adamas, the chief druid, or Silvandre, the philosopher of love). As lines of influence within the text's thematic plan begin to converge, and inasmuch as the society's religion is of pervasive importance, the question of religion and the undercurrent of ritual cannot be far from our minds.

The remaining perspective that might enhance our understanding of the textual role of disguise in the pastoral is the study of *sociological* effect. Within the textual world, the mask is able to bring about (in varying degrees of stability) the changing of social class, the crossing of otherwise intransigent barriers of caste. It may do so to adjust the social unit to meet new needs — needs of members to change lifestyle, or needs of society as a whole to fill in gaps in its hierarchy. It may be called into play to serve the social purposes of good or evil characters. Whatever its status, the mask is of interest for what it does to the society within the text and for the commentaries which it stands to make on the extratextual society in which the text is produced.

It is from these points of view, mindful of the generic history cited, that we propose to study the motif of disguise and the general phenomenon of identity in France's greatest pastoral romance. This is not to imply that our examination of the text will proceed according to an outline of four or five different methodologies; rather it is to say that our reading of the text will be enlightened and prodded by different sources of inquiry as we attempt to arrive at a full understanding of a complicated issue. This said, let us move on to associate generic conventions to disguise and identity as they are worked out in the text at hand.

The observation must be made that, at first glance, disguises in the pastoral narrative tradition might seem gratuitous, or even vapid, to readers initiated in the literary traditions of realism. Disguises are, after all, quickly donned or shed, and they do produce most extraordinary effects when judged against the standards of other narrative pacts. Implausible as they are, disguises here must be seen in relation to the genre of pastoral romance which engenders them, if they are to be appreciated for their textual value. In other words, they are created for certain effects related to the narrative, created to function within the fictive world of the narrative. Obvious as this aesthetic detail is, it tells us something about the genre on the whole and the text in particular. The world the reader is invited to enter is one where such disguise can easily be brought off — precisely for the reason that this world has a measure of the fantastic about it. And nothing is gratuitous in such a world. Characters are experiencing life and love there for the first time and, it is assumed, this romanesque world will be new to the reader as well. Two thousand years of pastoral tradition notwithstanding, the desired narrative effect is to portray a fresh world, and certainly not to offer a world view of the familiar or mundane.

Four very important generic conventions pertinent to disguise should be made clear at this point. First is the fact that, in the pastoral, identity is not a function merely of name or even of family membership. It also involves status and situation in a social unit. Likewise it involves affiliation along the moral axis of good/evil, heroic/villainous, supportive of the accepted code of love/not supportive, and so on. In short, characters are identified and known within society not only by name and ancestry, but by their beliefs and customary conduct as well. Consider in *L'Astrée* the case of Silvandre who comes to the society from without, ignorant of his familial origins, and is adopted by the circle of shepherds. For lack of other parameters, such as a past, an inheritance, personal associations, or even a beloved at the outset, he establishes his identity with what he has — his education, his wisdom and his platonic code of love.

A second point to be made about the genre is that characters labor under a kind of visual shortcoming which endows clothing or superficial physical change with the power to conceal identity and to create the illusion of otherness. Disguise is easy and most effective, and it must be said that faces count for less than clothes in attempts at identification and recognition.

The third important convention of the pastoral is that the disguise or mask is not inert — it tends to bring certain characteristics of the illusory identity with it. Characters like Felismena in the *Diana* and many before and after her who disguise as members of the opposite sex, assume traits of the opposite sex's comportment, strengths, weaknesses and other attributes taken in the text's *Weltanschauung* to be proper to the opposite sex; and this applies to male and female characters alike. The conventional implication is that sexual identity has something to do with how others perceive a character.

The remaining generic convention to be considered is that disguise in itself is not taken to be inimical to *truth* and hence evil or wrong. On the contrary, it often has the encouragement of the society's moral spokespersons. Like the literary text which is neither true nor false, the disguise is held to be neither truth nor falsehood. Rather it is a means to an end, whose morality is judged in light of that end.

Recognition, it should be noted, is thus by no means an automatic, reflex phenomenon in the pastoral. Recognition in relationships presupposes expectation: characters tend to recognize with certainty only other characters whom they have repeatedly seen recently and whom they are *likely* to encounter in their routine activities. Persons known but unexpected cannot count on being recognized, and the same holds for those who have been absent from the social unit for some time. By the very same token, disguise is rendered greatly effective by the fact that it presents an image that is unexpected. In light of this, the psychology of recognition is complex within the text, certainly unlike that in the extratextual world where perception and recognition are customarily more closely related. Within the pastoral, sight must be supported or validated by some other mechanism of memory, and memory must often be jogged by some mark of identity other than facial, such as a scar or a birthmark.

What is curious in *L'Astrée* and in most other pastoral narrative literature, is that the fictive society remains oblivious to the unreliability of facial recognition, and hence is easily taken in, time and again, by disguise. Pastoral characters remain unimpressed by their habitual inability to attribute identity properly with all but the most familiar of their acquaintances. This, of course, makes for a textual world of stylized confusion which can be exploited for purposes of narrative effect; but to go beyond the obvious effect of such a device, one can also detect the creation, within the tradition of the pastoral genre, of a world in which society is handicapped in its use of signs at a most elementary level. This is a society left to develop a reliable method of identifying friend and foe when it is deprived of means that readily serve the textual societies of, say, the novels of "realism." The thematic problem in question is fundamentally a semiotic one: the association of meaning with the outward marker. It is a problem at which pastoral societies work in interesting ways.

Characters ultimately seek clarity in identification, and not only for the obvious advantages of simplifying their personal lives. More is at stake: these are societies built on heroic values one of which is the accepted worth of the fixed hierarchy of Nature, the social hierarchy included. When social distinctions become blurred, as they tend to do in later pastoral romances, society must work at clarifying the social order (as, for example, occurs in *L'Astrée* with the creation of a new social class of "noble shepherds").

An unlikely device sometimes called upon to help establish identity is disguise itself. We shall later see particular illustrations of this function of the mask but for the moment, we are interested in the general thematics of disguise. Characters do indeed turn to the mask in attempts to give precision to the meaning which their peers associate with them. For heroic characters — those who espouse the heroic values — especially, the mask is a test of fortitude and endurance: it hides an identity that is a force within calling for recognition and respect from others. This interesting aspect of the mask dates back to Homer, as Sheila Murnaghan points out with respect to Odysseus whose disguise "represents the ability to endure a suspension of recognition — both in the narrow sense of recognition of identity, and in the broader sense of recognition of achievement and status..."[10]

We have said that the mask and false identities are not inert. They can take on a life of their own, both as the character interacts with them, and as they sometimes become counterproductive. In an atmosphere where recognition is difficult, masks usually create confusion where there was none previously. As matters of thematic interest, then, masks create new problems, sometimes greater than the difficulties they were intended to address. Recognition within the senses is simply too fallible in the pastoral world for the mask to be an easy success.

What makes matters more complex is the fact that pastoral societies are not saddled with problems of recognition seated solely within the senses. The universe around them works to create circumstances apt to confound Javert himself. For one thing, the figure of the double is well represented in this literature, exacerbating difficulties of identification and facilitating the efforts of those who would play on those difficulties. In some cases, as with Lydias and Ligdamon in *L'Astrée*,

---

[10] See Sheila Murnaghan, *Disguise and Recognition in the* Odyssey (Princeton: Princeton University Press, 1987) 5.

the physical resemblance is quite exact, yet the characters are not at all related by blood — indicating circumstances where extraordinary coincidence does its part to obfuscate the identity system. This is, of course, not to mention the many cases where family resemblance works against clarity in identification. Indeed, the appearance of the double is a stock device in the narrative pastoral tradition to the point where it illustrates readily the notion of an intrusive supernatural force that overlooks the shepherds' lives. In any event, the figure of the double is exploited in the pastoral, and for the same sorts of effects, as it is in other forms of literature of the fantastic.

Another problematic case, quite evident in the pastoral corpus of works, is the figure of the androgyne. The issue revolves around the question of sexual identity, and sexuality is a facet of identity which is traditionally ambiguous and loose in the pastoral. John T. Cull's fine article on the subject of androgyny in the Spanish pastoral narrative tradition is very thorough in presenting evidence of androgyny as *topos* dating back to antiquity.[11]

This literary figure is pertinent to the study of identity for two reasons. First, it is a play on the devices of character recognition: other characters are fooled, true identities are masked, etc. But perhaps more importantly, it calls into question (often obviously, as in *L'Astrée* and in the earlier Spanish pastoral novels) the particular character's sexual identity or inner nature, as well as the social unit's understanding of sexuality in general. Furthermore, as Cull points out, the establishment or discovery of a character's true identity often coincides with his or her marriage, which permanently redefines and clarifies the character's sexuality and puts androgyny aside. Clearly, then, androgyny and identity have much to do with one another.

The pastoral tradition in general, as well as *L'Astrée* in particular, portray this sort of imprecision in sexual identity as quite a natural phenomenon. The characters in question are young, discovering themselves and their erotic natures for the first time, in what is always depicted as the innocence and ingenuousness of youth. Their physical beauty is invariably described as one which would befit a member of either sex; this, of course, is a mechanism used to facilitate the use of transvestism in disguise. From Longus up through the Renaissance, pastoral narrative makes it a point to bring the two sexes

---

[11] John T. Cull, "Androgyny in the Spanish Pastoral Novels," *Hispanic Review* 57 (1989) 317-334.

together thematically by breaking down many of the barriers of biological distinction that would separate them otherwise.[12]

This appears in the novel as a quite natural phenomenon — an outward manifestation of a two-sided nature of sexuality in youth. This, again, is a youth in which sexuality has not yet settled into maturity and precision. That this is a commonplace in the pastoral is well established; but it should also be noted that the notion of the androgynous nature of humanity has roots in the very same ideological soil from which springs the pastoral code of love. In Plato's *Symposium* which, along with the dialogue *Phaedrus*, incorporates the entire platonic philosophy of love, the matter of androgynous nature is dealt with at some length. To Aristophanes is attributed therein a substantial and serious speech that outlines a human ontology, supposing the existence of a third sex that was to have been a union of male and female, possessed of a double nature. Aristophanes theorizes that the origins of the human species involved three sexes — male, female and the hermaphrodite. All of this last group were to have been divided in half by Zeus in an effort to control them; subsequently, each half instinctively sought its other half out of love. Aristophanes concludes that "...this love is always trying to reintegrate our former nature, to make two into one, and to bridge the gulf between one human being and another." Consequently, it is the descendants of this androgynous race who pursue heterosexual love, according to this theory; descendants of the male and female races, on the other hand, are homosexually inclined.[13]

This theory is neither endorsed nor refuted by Socrates in the dialogue, so it cannot be truly considered an integral part of the platonic code of love. Nonetheless, it does make an important step which we cannot afford to ignore in light of Plato's great and literal influence on pastoral authors up to and including d'Urfé. It makes of androgyny a phase of transition on the way of love, a phase to be recapitulated in the lives of individual pastoral characters who are in the process of defining their sexuality and their love for the first time. Thus it offers to the crafters of the pastoral tradition — who turned to Plato directly for the sum of their highly codified thematics of love — a theory of the attraction between the sexes which relates to the origins of the species. As pastoral literature shows us from antiquity up to

---

[12] See Cull, in note 11 above, for ample illustration of this point.
[13] *The Collected Dialogues of Plato* (New York: Pantheon, 1961) 543-544.

the seventeenth century, some form of this theory is brought into play time and again for young characters who pass through an androgynous identity on their way toward an unambiguous sexuality. And most often, disguise plays a role in this transition process.

2. An Overview of Disguise in *L'Astrée*

We turn our attention now to *L'Astrée*, to questions of identity and the mask as they appear in this great example of pastoral romance in the French baroque. It would seem self-evident that the motif of disguise and illusion is central to a work in which the very first episode of action stems from the motif, and in which disguise functions regularly as such a catalyst. Indeed, it is only on the second page of an enormous text that the reader of *L'Astrée* is made aware of the illusion created by the central characters, Celadon and Astrée, in order to allay suspicions of their own romantic relationship (I, 10). The only developmental information conveyed by the narrator prior to this first disguise is the pastoral's geographical setting, the introduction of the two characters as lovers, and the fact that they have been betrayed by a certain Semyre (which betrayal, in its own turn, involves another illusion as cited explicitly in the text):

> ...d'autant que Celadon desireux de *cacher* son affection, pour *decevoir* l'importunité de leurs parents..., s'efforçoit de *monstrer* que la recherche qu'il faisoit de ceste bergere estoit plustost commune que particuliere. *Ruse* vrayement assez bonne, si Semyre ne l'eust point malicieusement *desguisée*, fondant sur ceste *dissimulation* la trahison dont il deceut Astrée,... (I, 10; italics added)

If only by virtue of its proximity to the very outset of so huge a work, this passage is particularly meaningful to us since, first, it establishes early on the dynamism of the element of disguise which will often reappear and, second, it posits (as our italics serve to show) an obvious semantic code of description that will double as a code of conduct for many characters. "Décevoir, cacher, ruse, déguisée, dissimulation, montrer," a code quite well developed for so early a stage in the narrative. Such an exposition could certainly not be gratuitous, given both the rhythm with which it unfolds and the strategic position it occupies as the first major thematic development in *L'Astrée*. As far as action is concerned, the aftermath of these two initial illusions of identity will motivate the love intrigue of the two central characters throughout four volumes of the work. Other latent functions of the motif will come to light as we proceed.

The notions of disguise and illusion are inseparable — the former being a subcategory of the latter, more general heading. We shall, for our purposes, speak of the two together, understanding disguise to be the act (on the part of a character) of bearing an identity other than his or her own, for any reason and to any degree. Therefore, we shall consider equally under this rubric the case of Filidas whose father (for reasons of his own) raises her to adulthood in the manner and garb of a male (I, 197), as well as the "dame incognue" (I, 57-59) who carries the disguise motif to its extreme by substituting total anonymity for her identity in her dealings with Alcippe. In that such examples involve an illusion in the treatment of identity — the second one to the point where the "dame" would have Alcippe (as well as an otherwise omniscient storyteller, Celadon) believe that she has no nominal or visible identity at all — in that the truthful communication of name or qualitative information on the true self is hindered, we shall assume that the mechanics of disguise are in effect and can be studied as such.

A distinction that we are drawing may come under scrutiny: how may we speak of feigned conduct as disguise? After all, it is true in such a case as the example of Celadon and Astrée just cited that, in the strictest sense, there is no play on the actual identity of character as it is conventionally understood (recognition by name, for example): Celadon does not attempt to pass for another person in his feigned love of Aminthe (I, 150). Here the issue of how other characters "name" him does not come into question, since he is known to them and makes no attempt to alter his physical aspect. However, the disguise in this instance does not involve the physical aspect. Rather it is a metaphysical disguise, a disguise of an element of character which appears more perceptibly than the physical aspect to the society in *L'Astrée*. At issue here is an important character's outward declarations of love, as much or more a component of identity than anything else in this textual world. The name of Celadon in particular becomes a sign of fidelity in love; therefore, for Celadon to create the illusion of love for one other than Astrée is tantamount to changing his identity.

We use this example of role playing to illustrate the point of disguise because it is perhaps the starkest manifestation of typology by conduct in *L'Astrée*. The reader throughout knows very little (if anything at all) of Celadon's basic physical makeup, and this is a tradition of the pastoral which d'Urfé incorporates. Celadon is never described as tall or short, fair or dark. As concerns the visible, he is left in vagueness. One knows only that, at the outset, he wears his hair "rather long" (I, 16), and that while he subsequently lives the life of a hermit, he becomes emaciated and grows a beard (I, 487; II, 273). He, like all the other characters in the work, is not recognized primarily by the eye — for friends or reader — and becomes a type through his consistency in behavior. Known thus to all as a type of fidelity, Celadon finds a most effective mask in feigned conduct. The disguise calls into question so basic an element in the character's nature, that the perpetrator of the trickery (Astrée) is herself tricked.

The generic conventions of the pastoral (up through the baroque) are such that physical description is downplayed to the point of transparency, in favor of behavioral typology. This is indeed one explanation for the frequency of the motif of disguise. A work in which characters fail to recognize each other's faces, and in which a change of clothing can effect disguise even across sexual lines, lends itself most readily to the peripeties and games of disguise. And, of course, in a work where characters take so unequivocal a stance along thematic parameters (as Celadon and Silvandre, for example, align themselves on the side of constancy in love), it is easy to see how disguise can quickly become an effective motif. The combination of the misinterpretation of the mask, on the one hand, and the typological extremes of character, on the other, provides a wealth of material for the pastoral to exploit.

Heroes in pastoral literature align themselves, as we have suggested, on the side of what we may refer to as the pastoral ethic — the set of moral standards which the shepherd society accepts as its code of positive values, namely, fidelity in neoplatonic love, commitment to the principles of virtue and the good, and the acceptance of a very courtly code of civility and valor. In so doing, they find themselves actively engaged in the pursuit of truth. Be it truth in love, or the true realization of this ethic in a more general sense, the ideal of the "good shepherd" always entails a kind of crusade against the deceit of the antagonist, in a single-mindedness which does honor to the hero's character type. But a curious tanglement sets in with respect to the means through which this end is sought: as Jacques Ehrmann (72-86) (and Jean Rousset[1] before him) noted, disguise and illusion always seem to accompany the quest for the true — this quest which is a great motivation of action. Deceit is the lantern held out in search of the truth. The convention of the genre has it that, as Rousset explains, "On n'atteint au vrai qu'en prenant le détour de l'artifice" (Rousset 33).

Ehrmann associates illusion and truth as two necessary elements for the unfolding of a love relationship within the confines of the pastoral society. The masking of affection is ostensibly required by *honor* for the women in this society: female characters repeatedly bemoan the mores of men who supposedly have a marked tendency to enhance the reputation of their own prowess at the expense of women's honor, or else simply to take advantage of the women out of some inherent penchant for malice. For the moment, we must overlook the apparent disparity between this low opinion of men and the same men's general adherence to the code of courtly, neoplatonic love. Nonetheless, one statement of wariness is proffered in the desperate declaration of Dorinde, who says of the courtship of men:

> Mais pourquoy toutes ces peines et tous ces artifices? Pour plaire enfin à celles qu'ils veulent gaigner, et apres les pouvoir tromper, ou plutost les faire mourir de regret et d'ennuy de leurs perfidies et de leurs trahisons. (IV, 163)

Dorinde's language here is, of course, couched in the code of disguise and illusion. So it is to be expected, since "artifice" is the supposed weapon of men in their attack upon the virtue of womankind, that womankind respond with a "disguise" of its own. Such is not always the case; however, the hiding of any true emotion is one recourse available to the shepherdess who fears that a suitor may dupe her. As Ehrmann concludes, the love intrigue of the text is essentially a game of disguises. Man, tainted by the original sin of illusion, must overcome the responding illusion put forward by woman — and his counter often involves some sort of disguise. But at any rate, man

---

[1] J. Rousset, *La Littérature de l'âge baroque en France* (Paris: Corti, 1953) 33.

is habitually poor at communicating his intentions, and in this we note a basic problem in the recognition of traits of identity.

It becomes a case of fighting fire with fire, of fighting illusion with illusion for the sake of overcoming illusion and suppressing its effects. In this regard, the love intrigue of *L'Astrée* is a sort of microcosm of the sociopolitical conflict in the pastoral world: in this world fraught with the dangers of illusion and falsehood, the heroic undertake a platonic quest for the Good, but by paradoxically using disguise as a just means toward that end. In this text, matters are made worse since the society has (temporarily, at least) lost the services of its only objective barometer of truth — the Fontaine de Vérité et d'Amour. Hence the society is left to grapple with illusions in love, and by extension, in life, with whatever resources it can muster. Systematically it turns to the realm of illusion for the answer: feigned behavior, masked emotions, double-talk, and of course, disguise.

Illusion is required of woman by social constraint, and of man by social necessity. The confusion arises for the characters in that truth and illusion become inextricably entangled, all the while in the pursuit of the Good, to the point where it is difficult to discern which one is serving the purposes of the other. Nowhere is this more obvious than at the point in the text where Adamas, the chief druid and the character closest to being the incarnation of moral authority, persuades Celadon to adopt disguise in order to circumvent the letter of Astrée's law (II, 396-399). Thus it is Adamas, the personification of the quest for truth on the part of the pastoral society, who verbalizes the paradox in question — the truth of illusion, the realness of identity projected by disguise. In answer to Celadon's objection, Adamas responds: "...elle ne vous a pas deffendu d'estre Celadon, mais seulement de luy faire voir Celadon. Or elle ne vous verra pas en vous voyant, mais Alexis" (II, 398). The disguise assumes a reality of its own in this text, as much a reality as any other so-called truth which is accepted as such in the absolute. In its effort to bring the truth to light, the vehicle of illusion is almost a part of that truth itself.

It is Adamas who stands ostensibly as somewhat of a symbol for all that is genuine. We are told explicitly that his name derives from the Latin word for "diamond" (III, 646), an indication of obviously cratyllic value. It is he who repeatedly condemns the fakery of Climante who poses as a druid (see III, 703). Adamas is the interpreter of the oracles, and he is most qualified in the eyes of all the others to speak on behalf of the gods. But it is curious that he is a druid with a Latin name, in a Gallic society that is in ethnic tension with Rome. And so it is that this same guardian of truth materially aids Celadon in the "ruze" of disguise on two separate occasions (I, 383 and II, 398) — in the second case, as perpetrator and apologist of the illusion.

We have seen that illusion, disguise and trickery are woven into the fabric of the pastoral tradition dating back to antiquity. The point here is that this is even more the case in *L'Astrée*, to the degree where, from one perspective, truth and illusion can scarcely be distinguished. Ehrmann offers two explanations for this phenomenon. The first is that characters are entirely subject to the dicta of love, which by its nature distorts perception and reason. Ehrmann writes: "Dans le domaine des passions aucune certitude n'est possible. L'amour commence par affecter les sens puis 'l'entendement'" (Ehrmann 74). Love, having deformed the images of self and others in the eyes of characters, renders all judgmental objectivity impossible.

Ehrmann's second explanation is equally interesting, having to do with temporality and consciousness: in the characters, the consciousness of reality is somewhat compartmentalized to either the past, in nostalgia, or the future, in intuition. Illusion is thus temporally "localized" to the present as a kind of posited immediate (Ehrmann 75). Reality is either the remembrance of things past or the promise of things to come, either the legacy of previous generations and their covenant with the deity, or the new conditions the lovers seek to create for themselves. In between the two, the society remains in the realm of illusion with one eye to the future, and one to the past.

Of these two arguments, the latter is more compelling for the individual text at issue, since the former may be subsumed by reference to the pastoral tradition. Indeed, two further considerations may shed more light on the strange merger between truth, and illusion which is offered as truth. First is quite simply the matter of generic convention. The fact is that disguise, trickery and illusion in general were key motifs in the tradition of the romance since its origins. Convention made them stock stuff in the romance, to the point where they are as real and effective as any other textual reality. Accepted by convention as bearing such influence, the entire notion of illusion enjoys an efficacy that borders on the mystical. In *L'Astrée*, one need only consider the episode at the entrance of Climante's temple to see the point (see IV, 21 ff. and IV, 655 ff.). Here the power of illusion rivals the power of the divine, even in the minds of those who know that Climante is a fraud. But the genre is such that the narrator may set forth the illusion (for example, doors which close by themselves) without explaining until later the machinations, thus endowing the illusion with realness enough to convince characters who are both devout and informed.

Climante, much like the master narrator of the text, creates an illusion and makes it real in the relative sense. Climante's magic involves making a mechanism of human invention seem like a genuine work of the gods. The master narrator, on the broader level of the text, has his own "magic" of making the fiction real for his readers. This is, of course, the case with any instance of narrative fiction. However, the genre of romance arms the narrator with an additional tool: to the same extent that he can speak the fiction as true, he can create illusions within the confines of this fiction, and have them taken for reality in the action related by the text. The genre, as a matter of convention (and for its participation in the fantastic), permits the interchanging of divine (or "real") and illusory magic — to the confusion of the characters, we might add. In a text where the rational and the fantastic coexist as a matter of basic definition, such as in the pastoral romance, one can fully expect that illusion will be "raised" to the status of reality and thereby enjoy an equality of verisimilitude. Thus the lines of demarcation between the two become hazy, aided simply by the fact that the genre of the text permitted it to be so.

The second explanation which we offer for the confusion of truth and illusion deals with the ethical system of the society. The fact is that the society as a whole never calls this ethical code into question, never challenges its authority or rectitude. The system itself, for its part, precludes such a challenge to its bases, deriving its constitution from the gods, through their duly appointed vicars and interpreters. The society in the aggregate accepts this moral order (along with the attendant sociopolitical order) in its totality: the society is, generally speaking and in platonic terms, in quest of the Good and the true.

Why then are there so many illusions and disguises in the action? It is precisely because the society's collective ends are never in doubt that there is no restriction on the means used to achieve those ends. It matters little that trickery and disguise are incompatible with truth in the purest sense: the fact that the ultimate intention is toward the Good provides justification on the moral plane. Likewise, it is unimportant if disguise and illusion are principal weapons in the arsenal of the text's few villains: the rain falls on the just and the unjust, and the final reckoning is reserved for the end of the pastoral. What is important is that the heroes be true to society's goals as well as to their own. Consequently, a lover must work toward the fulfillment of his or her love, a noble must work toward the perpetuation of the proper social order, etc. Should disguise and illusion become useful to these proper ends, they pose no moral problem for the collective social conscience. The fact that there is a logical discrepancy is overlooked by the society,[2] and the fact that there is no moral discussion is tantamount to dismissal of any moral issue.

This brand of moral relativism permeates *L'Astrée* and the pastorals of the late Renaissance. With regard to the moral code, it is clear that the conscience of the lover is the principal effective barometer of ethics — at least as far as sexual morality is concerned. Indiscretions, jealousy and illusion become the trappings of true affection. Some "offences" committed in the name of love are chided only superficially and are quickly brushed aside by a light-hearted pardon from the beloved. So integral are they to the love intrigues of the novel that they could not possibly be taken for evil (again, according to whatever socio-ethical conscience is set forth in the text); for, as Rousset observes:

> ...rien de plus masqué que ces coeurs simples; le combat contre l'artifice se livre à grands coups d'artifice. C'est que nous ne sommes pas au XXe siècle, mais au temps du Bernin: les vêtements ou les voiles composent les corps, les masques se confondent avec les visages, le décor passe pour l'édifice;... (Rousset 33).

In the later pastoral romance, love is not the subject of true philosophizing or moralizing, but rather it is idealized. The fact that the pastoral, as a genre, hardly offers its setting or characters as real forests or shepherds is certainly one indication of this. Love, like setting or character, is an ideal phenomenon in the text which answers to no law but its own. If, as in *L'Astrée*, it is postulated that love will function as the omnipotent prime-mover of so much action, then it is easy to see how the question of "right or wrong" loses most of its force in the face of the irresistible. It is for this reason that we may dispense with the assertion of Ehrmann (91-92) that there are two distinct moralities of love set out in the text, and may reduce the ques-

---

[2] Consider as an example the case of Celadon who violates the rules of the temple by disguising himself as a woman in order to judge Astrée in the beauty contest, and thereby to further his own romantic interest. He, of course, has the tacit approval of Astrée, as well as that of the scriptor, and no moral issue is brought to bear (see I, 114 ff.).

tion to simpler terms: two effective moral codes on the metaphysical level would amount to no code at all, and this is why Ehrmann is at a loss to discern the position of d'Urfé on these moral grounds. Simply stated, d'Urfé is best considered the novelist, and not the moralist, by the critical reader of his text.

L'Astrée, for all of its polemics, cannot accurately be considered as a philosophical document. The tensions which are at work in the text are of a nature other than the ideological. The work is, of course, abounding in contradictions of what would be its central thesis of neo-platonic love, were the latter to be taken seriously as a cogent doctrine.[3] But even on the level of action within the text — much less at any social level outside the text — the ideology and erudition of love are quite sterile and ineffectual in the working out of that action. Clifton Cherpack makes a compelling case for this point, as he asks:

> How can the reader be expected to take seriously ideas and theories which are set forth at length but often contradicted and which are ultimately nullified by the omnipotence of mysterious and occasionally capricious forces? No help in this matter is to be had from the narrator who is telling this story in the first person. He occasionally intervenes to make brief comments, but he never gives any indication of what is to be believed.[4]

Thus it is clear that the didactic reading of *L'Astrée* is not the best of all possible readings, for lack of a harmony between action and the motif of Platonic debate on the subject of love. To the same extent, a study of the motif of disguise should not stall at the point of whatever moral issue is made of it in the text. To say that this motif principally points up the tension between truth and illusion (a facet of the moral problematic) is, at best, misleading since morality is no more coherently worked out in the text than is the philosophy of love. So let us move on, then, to consider disguise in its role within the text as it contributes to and illuminates other tensions and oppositions there.

As stated above, we shall consider as disguise any misrepresentation of information pertaining to the identity of the true self. This

---

[3] See also Laurence A. Gregorio, "Implications of the Love Debate in *L'Astrée*," *French Review* 56.1 (October 1982) 31-39 for discussion of this point in detail.
[4] Clifton Cherpack, "Form and Ideas in *L'Astrée*," *Studies in Philology* 69.3 (July 1972) 327.

misrepresentation can be voluntary or involuntary, calculated or accidental, whole or partial, physical or nominal, and can transcend sexual and social barriers. We shall take all such cases into consideration, since all involve the functioning of the literary motif of the mask, the alteration of character identity. Thus our study of the motif will be based on the notion of impairment in the communication of name or qualitative information regarding this identity. In semiotic terms, disguise is defined for our purposes as the interruption of direct correlation between signifier and signified of character.

This would all seem rather straightforward and perfectly clear were it not for one troublesome area. What of the complicated variety of illusion which is caused by feigned conduct in the context of love? The difficulty here arises, of course, out of the singular role which the whole notion of love plays as part of the very foundation of the text. How are we to account for the unique situation of a common illusion whose dynamism and far-reaching efficacy bring about so much action and cause so much confusion for characters?

The fact is that, as often occurs in the pastoral tradition, many characters in *L'Astrée* exist primarily as lovers. When such characters are not actively involved in the pursuit of their amorous ends, they are usually expounding on theories of love, or listening to the narration of someone else's love story. These characters, who are obviously in the majority in *L'Astrée*, are functions of their romantic interest: they are as they love. When asked, Who is Silvandre? most readers would respond that he is the theoretician of constancy in love. Likewise asked of Hylas, one would undoubtedly answer that he is the type of the inconstant lover, and so on through much of the cast of characters.

One would be hard put to deny that love is far and away the dominant theme (though again we emphasize, not a coherent philosophical system). To say that most of the text's characters are preoccupied with love (or talking about love) would be something of an understatement. Love is the catalyst responsible for their actions. Coupled with the phenomenon of narrative, it is the very stuff of their existence. If they perpetuate themselves (and the text) through the telling of stories, then it must be admitted that the matter of this storytelling is the untiring and ubiquitous love intrigue.

In keeping with the generic tenets of the romance, most characters of *L'Astrée* are not developmental. If they advance in experience, it is by reaffirming beliefs that they held at the outset. They are fixed in the time of the text as inveterate lovers. In all candor one must agree that they serve little other purpose to the action narrated. Likewise, one should keep sight of the fact that this voluminous text they spin has always, since its creation, been received by its readership as a basis for the precious idealization of love. The idealization, the personification of love seem to be the ostensible motivating interests of most characters.

Silvandre, Celadon and a host of others simply would not be understood as they are, if they did not love or theorize about love. Given this essential quality in the characterization of the work, it is safe to make certain postulates. One is that love thus constitutes an important element of the inner being or "être" of character in L'Astrée. How a character loves and whom he or she loves are more significant pieces of information within the text (as well as to the reader) than name or physical identifying characteristics. Quite simply, characters are known to each other and even to themselves by measures set on romantic scales. Celadon would not be Celadon if he did not love Astrée and only Astrée. Hence our basic understanding of the text would be greatly altered if this relationship were suddenly to change. Celadon is what he is and does what he does because he loves Astrée, and the text abounds with other such love relationships.

Another assumption that we may therefore make is that love forms a central means of identification, and that any effort to misrepresent a romantic relationship constitutes a disguise which, within the text, is as real as any change of name or physical appearance. If love is part of the "être" of character, then feigned love is a mask, an untrue identity.

For this reason, we shall include the notion of feigned love in our study of the motif of disguise, and treat it as we would any other misleading representation of identity. We assess it to be a change of identification brought about not through physical means, but instead through behavioral means.

There is a variety of disguise types in L'Astrée, born of varying motivations and assumed to varying degrees. The spectrum is fully displayed throughout the work, and its end result is a penetrating exploration of many of the motif's possibilities. For closer scrutiny let us divide the overall motif of disguise into the categories that the text seems to offer in logical organization. The first and largest rubric is that of physical disguise, which itself must be subdivided. Under this heading we consider: the change of identity via the creation of new identity (the means being transsexual disguise, disguise across lines of social class, and more inert, substitutive disguise whose function is simply that of the mask); the exchange or the unilateral assumption of preexisting identity without the creation of any new identity; and, the mask which itself is inert and whose function is to withhold identity totally without substituting another identity. For the sake of unity, we consider all of the cases of transsexual disguise together, even though a small number of them involve the assumption of preexisting identities.

Our second rubric of disguise is the behavioral variety already mentioned. We include in this category the only type of conduct which really effects change of identity for characters in a pastoral romance, feigned love. After these two larger areas, there remain categories of disguise that are turned to only infrequently in the text. They are the disguise we refer to as nominal (that in which the identity of name is mistaken), and finally, the mask borne with intent other than to deceive (differing from previously mentioned disguise types only in the absence of the motive of deception). These last two categories account for a mere six cases of disguise combined — a fact which graphically indicates the text's and the genre's propensity for disguises of physical or behavioral nature.

From this point, we proceed to the study of individual cases, illustrations of categories of disguise delineated above. In the interest of concision, and conscious of the fact that an exhaustive survey could be deadly to the reader, we do not include all cases of disguise in the body of our work, foregoing the study of those relatively few (about a dozen) cases which turn out to be repetitive or thematically insignificant. Our intention is to make plain the major tendencies in the motif of disguise while giving principal attention to a limited number of instances. First, we look at the highly conventionalized phenomenon of *travestissement*.

3. *Travestissement*

As sheer numbers go, the physical disguises far outweigh all the other forms of game-playing in the sphere of identity. The margin of numerical superiority is roughly two to one over the other types of disguise combined. The first type we are about to investigate is perhaps the most interesting the genre has to offer: disguise across sexual lines.

Of the twelve such cases found in the first four volumes of *L'Astrée*, we shall examine seven individually. The disguises chosen for study here are those that are of most substance and consequence; those not chosen offer little development of the motif. In any case, we shall look at the masks in the order of their appearance in the text.

As might be expected by a reader familiar with Montemayor and d'Urfé's other Renaissance models, the first instance of transsexual physical disguise occurs relatively close to the beginning of *L'Astrée* (I, 114 ff.). It is the mask borne by the character Celadon who dresses as a shepherdess and assumes the original name of Orithie, thus creating a new identity. We note with interest that the first transsexual disguise is taken on by Celadon, a figure who, later in the text, will come to be characterized entirely by the motif. This disguise is narrated in the voice of Astrée who recounts the intercalated "Histoire d'Astrée et Phillis."

It occurs in something of a representation of the mythical tale of Paris and the golden apple: here Celadon adopts the mein of a shepherdess in order to mingle with the shepherd women who are segregated during a feast. By so doing, Celadon braves the punishment of stoning and flouts the strict interdiction of contact between the sexes, an interdiction taken quite seriously by the rest of the society. As the inevitable great coincidence would have it, Celadon (disguised) is elected to judge a beauty contest in which his beloved Astrée is a finalist. In exchange for awarding the first prize to Astrée, Celadon exacts from her a promise to afford whatever her judge will ask. At this point, Celadon reveals his true identity and abandons his first of several transsexual disguises.

Some points come to light in this first, simple case. To begin with, the disguise is assumed here for the express purpose of the furtherance of an erotic drive. Secondly, the means which are placed at Celadon's disposal (through the disguise) are actually an occasion of transgression with respect to the moral and social code — and yet, this code is set aside by Celadon. Despite the fact that he is ostensibly a highly moral character and quite concerned with the observance of the social order, he uses disguise to enter the women's temple, and he uses it further to dupe his beloved. All this he does for the sake of love which is obviously of higher priority than the society's stuffy mores at this point. Third is the fact that the disguise is of a very brief temporal duration, and it is a complete success both in its intended advancement of a love interest, as well as in its intended change of identity. And one other circumstance is clear: the moral wrong inherent in Celadon's use of transsexual disguise (i.e. violation of social code of segregation) is considered as secondary by Astrée, whose protests are admittedly pro forma.

This first of the text's many transsexual disguises is maintained only briefly, yet it is highly effective. The degree of disguise is total: Celadon "becomes" a woman to the extent that the lot falls to him to judge the ideal in feminine beauty. A new identity (a name) is assumed, but the story's narrator, Astrée, continues to designate him by his name and to speak of him in the masculine. Celadon's virility is here preserved under the disguise; it is important to note, however, that such is not the case in every instance of transsexual disguise, since frequently the assumption of the mask entails the adoption of the characteristics of that mask's gender. But the motivation for the disguise is amorous in nature, and the disguise itself clouds the vision of Astrée. Nonetheless, it must be noted that Astrée remains visually observant enough to notice that "il changea deux ou trois fois de couleur,..." (I, 115) upon seeing her in a state of undress. This change of color, as well as the "contentement" that Celadon experiences, are traits of the masculinity underlying the mask — traits that create explicit tension with the mask, but do not impair its effectiveness at all. And Astrée is capable of distinguishing nuances of facial expression, but remains blind to the more fundamental question of identity.

The second of the romance's transsexual disguises points up significant differences from the previous one. Here we are dealing with a mask that covers no previous identity — the mask itself serves as the bearer's first and enduring identity (I, 197 ff.). Initial motivation for the disguise is not romantic, as before, but economical instead: in order to reap the advantages of a marriage pact struck with Celion, Phormion makes it known that his newborn child is a boy; he plans to marry this "son" off to Celion's daughter, Diane, and thereby assure his offspring of Diane's inheritance. The child, Filidas, is thus raised as a boy and taught the pursuits thought proper to masculinity. The disguise, of course, is involuntarily borne at the outset, but this changes. Filidas, in a gesture of explicit revolt against the rigid material limits placed on the female sex, decides (when finally given the choice) to retain the mask as a permanent identity.

She keeps the disguise up until shortly before the end of her life, when she breaks down and confesses her love for a male character named Filandre. The twist is that, at this point, this Filandre and his sister have temporarily themselves swapped identities. The text sums up the situation: "A Filidas qui est fille, (Amour) fait aimer une fille…" (I, 212). Filidas' life arrives at a sad and violent end as she comes to the aid of Diane when the latter is assaulted by a man whom the text depicts in quite diabolical terms.

The differences between this disguise and the first are obvious with respect to chronological duration and ostensible intent of disguise. There is, however, another important distinction: we observed that the result of Celadon's first disguise across sexual lines was the advancement of his romantic interest; but the result of Filidas' disguise is only the confusion of her amorous pursuits. There would seem to be an implicit moral judgment on the part of the text, resulting from the contrasts of these two cases: transsexual disguise used only as a vehicle for the furtherance of love is acceptable and is rewarded; however, when it arises out of a motivation other than romantic, it is accompanied by the wholesale and life-long assumption of unnatural characteristics, it is unacceptable to the text's moral code, and it meets with its just retribution at the hands of a seemingly supernatural creature. In other terms, the text seems already to discriminate between ethical and unethical uses for the very same means, and to reward or punish them accordingly.

Filidas' *travestissement*, like all others, is total in physical degree. It is also successful in the achievement of its initial goal: fulfillment of the contract made between the two fathers. But the disguise's effectiveness later breaks down, and the outcome is a first hint that there exists a code of female behavior which cannot be broken without penalty. Virtually all of Filidas' femininity is repressed under the mask, and it would seem that she is castigated for this.

The next disguise has already come before us. It occurs simultaneously with the preceding case, and offers an interesting counterpoint to it. Filandre, in order to be closer to Diane, changes identity with his sister, thus exploiting a previously existing resemblance. The sister, Calirée, is only too glad to oblige, for this enables her to spend time away from her aged husband, and she agrees to cut her hair to enhance the disguise. The exchange of identity achieves its immediate purpose of bringing Filandre nearer to his beloved, but is rather shortlived since a well-meaning third party (Daphnis) reveals the disguise to Diane. Diane, outraged at first, forgives Filandre and Calirée (I, 209 ff.).

The opposition between the disguises of Filandre and Filidas stands out, if only for the reason that their names are so similar. Clearly juxtaposed in the text, they differ greatly. In the first place, the mask of Filandre is motivated by his love interest; that of Filidas is not. Then there is the matter of the intensity of disguise — the degree to which the bearer adheres to the mask. We have discussed how Filidas completely accepted the mask of manhood. Filandre, on the other hand, assumes only the physical appearance of femininity with none of the usual characteristics which the text associates with it. In this vein, we must note the fact that a double standard appears: in disguise as in many things, the text and its social code allow the male more latitude and less censure. Lastly we see that the disguise ultimately improves (however slightly) the position of Filandre in the sight of his beloved, where the same sort of disguise only confuses the difficult romantic situation of Filidas.

The two disguises come into contact in revealing fashion. Along with Diane, another "trompée" of Filandre's disguise is Filidas; the latter, in love with Filandre, declares her love to Calirée who is masquerading as Filandre. This serves only to underscore the pastoral's tacit judgment of the types of disguise: Filandre's masquerade as his sister is somehow more natural and worthy of success since it has the privileged status of serving an honorable love. There is no inherent transgression of the natural order in this case, and the mask is purely external. In the case of Filidas, however, the mask is internalized, intensified by volition, and the basic differences between the sexes (as far as society is concerned) are themselves called into question. In such a situation, the only possible result is the confusion of Filidas in life, and the absence of fulfillment in death — a death of dismemberment that graphically symbolizes her fragmented existence.

Filidas and Filandre are juxtaposed in name and in transsexual disguise, and so are they in death, for they both die at the hands of the same fiendish creature. But the distinctions which we have observed hitherto are again borne out. Filidas dies in a manner almost bereft of honor, certainly bereft of love. Filandre, conversely, achieves an ideal set out time and again throughout the text: he sacrifices his life for his beloved, he lives long enough to exchange vows of love with her, and he dies in the knowledge that she will honor and love his memory. He who pursued just ends (through the justifiable use of disguise across sexual lines) is again rewarded — and it is he who, in dying, slays the menacing attacker and preserves the life of the one he loves. So evidently there is a moral gradient that applies to disguise and runs parallel to the pastoral ethic: disguise intended for ends in harmony with heroic values is treated by narrator and society alike as justifiable, regardless of other moral ramifications; disguise that challenges the natural order (as so perceived by social standards) runs afoul of the pastoral ethic.

The next transsexual mask provides a variation to an already familiar theme. It is the second time that Celadon assumes the guise of a female, and again it is accompanied by the creation of a new identity and name (Lucinde). It is important to note also that this is one of the very few cases of upward social mobility in disguise: Celadon, a shepherd albeit of noble ancestry, is here pretending to be a nymph (I, 383-384 and 473).

This is the first disguise of gender which occurs not in the course of an intercalated narrative, but rather is recounted in the voice of the master narrator of *L'Astrée*. There is one significant narrative change that appears as a result of this break in the pattern established up to this point. The master narrator in his first treatment of transsexual disguise elects to add a new dimension to it by referring to the bearer in the linguistic feminine ("elle," "la," etc.) (I, 473 ff.) for the duration of the disguise. This disguise seems to take on a reality in the eyes of the narrator who calls the character Lucinde while the mask is in effect, and who goes so far as to recognize the sexual crossing in his discourse. This is the first example we have of a storyteller's participation in the disguise through his narrative language.

The mask assumed by Celadon is thus set apart from the others in the way that it is related by the narrative voice. It is distinctive in other ways, too. This is, for example, a transsexual disguise intended to effect escape from a romantic entanglement: Celadon is disguised as a nymph so that he may obtain leave from the principal nymph, Galathée, who is infatuated with him. Hence we observe the pressing into service of one of the ordinary machinations of the text's many lovers, with the purpose avoiding involvement in an amorous relationship of *mésalliance* that is judged improper by all except Galathée.

This disguise is also assumed by Celadon at the behest of Adamas, the chief druid and moral spokesman of the society. The fact that Adamas takes so active a role in the game of disguise is quite significant: in so doing he condones the practice, in effect, and thus there could be nothing inherently evil in a measure which he so wholeheartedly approves. But as we shall see, Adamas is not necessarily consistent, so his participation in this disguise is not tantamount to ethical endorsement on the absolute scale. Nonetheless, in relative terms it is to be understood that there is nothing necessarily unnatural in transsexual disguise: Adamas never calls the moral rectitude of the guise into question since, for him, the termination of an affair of misalliance is an end which would, under any circumstances, justify whatever means might be needed. Such a practical approach to the question is in keeping with Adamas' habitual rationalistic stance on the ethics of love and social codes (which stance itself is in marked opposition to the text's ostensible thesis of idealizing the romantic).[1]

The disguise achieves its end of facilitating Celadon's escape from the clutches of the principal nymph. The motivation of the bearer is one of propriety regarding the "natural" norms in the social code

---

[1] See, for example, Adamas' conversation with Celadon (I, 381) for an illustration of the rationalistic view of nature and love.

of love (set forth in the text in the voice of Celadon himself [I, 381]). The duration of the disguise is brief, as Celadon wears it only long enough to escape. Once this has occurred and the mask is dropped, the narrator returns to speaking of the character in the masculine.

The following mask of sexual identity is rather complex. It is the guise assumed by Melandre, a woman of noble extraction, for the ultimate purpose of assuring the safety of her beloved Lydias. This disguise becomes intricately entangled with the confusion of identity between this Lydias and his look-alike, Ligdamon — an inadvertent shift of identity which we shall later consider under another rubric. At any rate, the disguise of Melandre is a long-standing one (in narrative chronology) because it is recounted only in parts and by several narrative voices: first by Amasis (I, 459 ff.), next by Ligdamon (IV, 687 ff.), then by Lydias (IV, 760 ff.) and finally by Melandre herself (IV, 765 ff.).

As in the preceding case we considered (the disguise of Celadon as "Lucinde"), the disguise of Melandre entails a shift of gender in the narrative discourse: those secondary narrators just mentioned (except, of course, Melandre who speaks in the first person feminine) refer to her in the masculine during those parts of their narratives for which she is disguised as "Le Chevalier Triste." Seen thus in two successive cases, the gender change in narrative discourse is a clear effort on the part of the text to make more potent the motif of the mask, to reinforce its own traditions and codes. By referring to the character in question in the inappropriate gender, all of the narrators (including the text's master narrator) intensify the strength of the mask to deceive. They endow illusion with one more degree of the reality it seeks to displace, and the motif of disguise, specifically, becomes a principal power of illusion. The narrative shift, then, is something of a signal that illusion in general is a thematic keystone in *L'Astrée*, that characters often fall victim to illusion as they endeavor to define the identity of others and of themselves.

While the motivation of this disguise is love-related, it is not like those we have seen. Melandre assumes this mask in order to save the life of the one she loves, and not specifically to advance her standing in the beloved's sight (the latter being typically a ploy of male characters). This too is a stock type of disguise in the pastoral, often seen in Montemayor and the Italian romances. Rather than the erotic interest, there is, in this case, a more practical concern in play: unlike Celadon and the clownish Hylas who assume the guise of the opposite sex in order to gain access to sexually segregated proceedings, Melandre here is disguised in order to protect Lydias from the danger of a menacing third person. She subsequently maintains the disguise in order to take the place of Lydias in captivity.

Melandre becomes a man in the actual (textual) sense of assuming faculties which are properly masculine in the pastoral tradition, and exercising them with sufficient fortuitous success as to leave no doubt of the convincing nature of the disguise. She is able to fight Lipandas to a draw (I, 465), and later she comes to the rescue of Ligdamon in a trench (IV, 772) during a battle.

In light of the more complete crossing of gender lines, why does Melandre not meet with the same retribution that we saw in the case of Filidas? The answer is to be found, as one might expect, in the text's code of moral relativism. Filidas is "punished" for the unjustifiable use of disguise which, in and of itself, is not morally reprehensible; it is in her actions (read *intentions*) that is found the reversal of a basic moral order. Melandre's actions, on the other hand, may be justified by her laudable, love-inspired intentions. Furthermore, her disguise is only functional and does not betoken any revolt against the natural distinction of the sexes— "natural," of course, meaning "commonly accepted, socially understood." Melandre, unlike Filidas, exhibits no tendency to dissociate herself inwardly from her condition; on the contrary, she is quick to let her transsexual disguise fall when it has served its purpose. So it is the quest for change of essence which is doomed, whereas the change of appearance is an acceptable, effective tool.

The implication is significant, for it brings to light a structuring device for the motif of disguise. This motif turns on the notion of disparity between being and appearance, between "être" and "paraître." And now, underneath the mask, we see the same opposition at work: the "être" in the process of either redefining or reaffirming itself (Filidas and Melandre respectively) as it comes into tension with the external trappings of disguise. In the meantime, appearances carry along with themselves the physical capacities associated with them. Melandre can therefore make war like a man, but may not try to become one in the manner of Filidas, without the risk of suffering the consequences Filidas suffers.

Under this rubric of transsexual disguise, the case which is the most complex, the longest borne, and the best known of all the disguises of *L'Astrée* is that of Celadon who masquerades as Alexis, the daughter of Adamas. We are considering this under the present heading even though, in this case, there is no creation of a new identity in the strictest sense: a true Alexis is alluded to by the characters, although she is never encountered by the reader. At any rate, it is fitting that we treat this disguise here since its salient factor is the crossing of sexual lines of identity, and not the assumption of the persona of another significant character.

In duration this disguise is enormous, and it is far beyond the scope of all others in the text. Even that of Filidas, who lives a whole life of transsexual disguise, does not approach in narrative length this famous mask of Celadon (from II, 397 through the end of volume IV). Clearly it is the central disguise of all which are seen in the romance, if only by virtue of its long-standing and total effectiveness in obscuring identity. Certainly no disguise in the text is more pronounced or more complete.

The mask in question bears several significant similarities with some other disguises already considered. First is the fact that a shift in narrative discourse occurs through which the character is denoted by the grammatical forms of the feminine. The narrator is often quick to remind the reader explicitly that a change in the sign has taken place (II, 399).

The pattern that develops in this shift in narrative discourse is of great import here. At the outset of the disguise, the narrator is careful to call the character by his assumed name, Alexis, when he is in costume, and by his real name when he is not (see III, 13-14). At this point in the narrative some confusion arises in the gender which is linguistically attributed to Celadon (III, 24). This may be interpreted as stemming from the fact that the inner reality and the outer mask are not yet sufficiently reconciled to effect a harmonious change of identity. The reconciliation is not long in coming, for Celadon, after this point, is rarely seen out of the guise of Alexis and, as one might suppose, is almost uniquely referred to in the feminine.

However, as the disguise wears on, the tension, which reflects the conflict going on within Celadon, redevelops in this narrative denotation. His manhood, at first easily denied and disguised, later struggles its way to the surface, destined eventually to burst out of the restraints of that disguise. Celadon is willing at the outset to take on the aspect of womanhood, but as the mask becomes more and more difficult for Celadon to bear, the narrator allows this tension to be shown even on the level of language — sometimes within the confines of a single sentence, such as

> (Alexis) pensa plusieurs fois qu'il estoit temps de se declarer pour tel qu'*il* estoit, et de...desabuser (Astrée) de l'opinion qu'elle avoit qu'*elle* fust la fille d'Adamas... (IV, 796; italics added).

Of the time during which the narrative relates the story of Celadon, he spends the far greater part masquerading as a woman. The mask for him is something of a defense mechanism, a means of resisting the pressures or responsibility of manhood as it is defined by society (see Halladin's harangue to Damon [III, 31]). Celadon lives out a preference for the acceptable passivity of feminine identity, until his latent masculine identity demands recognition in later passages of the text. This is Celadon's character evolution: the realization of his own sexuality and the acceptance of the attendant duties of manhood, imposed as they are by social code. This is, as suggested above, mirrored in the narrative discourse where the feminine denotation dominates at first, only to be opposed by the masculine until the latter bursts forth in the battle sequence (IV, 798 ff.) and itself becomes dominant in the end.[2]

Another similarity with a past disguise of Celadon comes to light here: the fact that Adamas instigates and approves the disguise. In his quest for the achievement of the just end, the chief druid goes so far as to play word games with the letter and language of the "law" in question (Astrée's banishment of Celadon, see II, 396-398). This is, of course, the same Adamas who condemns the charades of a false druid, who prescribes strict adherence to ethical codes elsewhere in the text, and who himself functions in society as the interpreter of the pronouncements of the oracles. But here he goes to great pains to convince Celadon that the role-play is justifiable, persuading the shepherd to contravene the spirit of the law which, for the ideal lover, would be intransigent. Celadon is irresolute (a feminine trait in *L'Astrée*'s social code; see III, 31) and goes along with the ruse.

The younger Celadon goes further in his avoidance of masculine traits (again, as the textual society would define them) and in the ease with which he crosses lines of sexual identity. For example, he admits to Adamas a lack of courage (II, 396). So to what extent does he actually change sexual identity?

---

[2] Such a confluence of images of male sexuality and images of war should come as no surprise to readers versed in the chivalry of the Middle Ages.

In the first place, much is made of his efforts to pass for a woman physically, and of his striking resemblance to the daughter of Adamas. The role is so well rendered that Hylas, the ever amorous jokester, is taken to the point where he falls in love with the "feinte druide" (II, 464 and III, 66, for example). Celadon learns and observes the life of the druid women (II, 399), and fits into the female circle of the shepherd society. He goes so far in his role as to participate in the customary, almost ritual, feminine lamentation of the mores of men, as we shall later have occasion to note. However, the most noteworthy refusal of masculinity is the unchivalrous conduct implicit in his actions: twice he braves the "law" through transsexual disguise and legalistic semantics — first to escape Galathée, and here to circumvent Astrée's order of banishment.

All of this is conduct obviously unbecoming a man or a lover in the pastoral society which, in matters of ethics, is often depicted as an aristocracy superimposed on the rustic setting and governed by the code of chivalry. True, virtually all is regarded as fair in love; however, the responsibility to one's sexual identity is, if not totally overriding, certainly expected to be compatible with any endeavor he or she undertakes. But where disguise comes into play, the pastoral code equivocates — and this holds not only for d'Urfé, but in his generic sources as well. Ideally a male character may pursue the interests of love, all the while remaining faithful to the social code of masculine conduct, even if he should find it expedient to don the guise of femininity for a while. We have seen how the mask tends not to be unencumbered; the Celadon/Alexis disguise illustrates well how the mask can take the character beyond the ideal measure of moderation, and how it can become something of an "internalized" mask.

The structure of "être" vs. "paraître" beneath the disguise itself is evident in the conflict of Celadon's latent virility which finally wells up within him toward the end of the text. As we observed earlier, the tension of "être" vs. "paraître" is an interiorization of the same tension on which the motif of disguise is predicated: on the level of physical appearance, the true masculine identity of Celadon is hidden behind the feminine costume of Alexis; on a deeper level of character, his sexual identity is engaged in a struggle for realization with traits that the pastoral attributes to femininity as a matter of custom. But he is not reproached by the text's value system for the initial assumption of the aspect of femininity. This may be because it is by hiding his virility that he discovers it. It may also be because his intentions do nothing to challenge the natural order implicit in the pastoral ethic.

The Alexis mask is the epitome of the motif of disguise in *L'Astrée*. With one exception, only those who know of the disguise can see through it. That exception is the character Semire who is the original villain responsible for Celadon's banishment from the sight of Astrée.

Why Semire? One answer might propose that Semire provides a "coup de théâtre," a narrative twist. But there is another answer: Semire is the only villain of all who converts to the cause of the good; of course, he eventually pays with his life, but he lives to confess his guilt and to right his wrong. In his sacrifice of expiation, he is endowed with the vision which the rest of society lacks. He sees through the "Alexis" mask, and is thus able to transcend the illusion which is the stuff of disguise. It is as if the great act of sacrifice carries along with itself a perception that goes beyond appearances, beyond the games that mortals play. Yet it is a vision gained only as the character is about to die.

Seen in this light, the ontology of disguise in the text becomes more complex. On the one hand, it is an acceptable means to a just end, sanctioned by Adamas for justifiable ends, capable of advancing the all-important love interest, and so on. On the other hand, it can be a game, a petty pastime, humorous at times (as with Hylas), or done for enjoyment (III, 593-596, for example). The narrative therefore gathers quite divergent aspects of one and the same motif, presenting them in an unchanging manner. To the same extent to which the text incorporates both some serious neoplatonic discussion of love (with Silvandre et al.) as well as the living and speaking contradiction of same (Hylas), so the text also creates a serious storytelling tool in the motif of disguise, and at the same time pulls the props from under that seriousness.

This disguise of Celadon is across social as well as sexual lines, with upward social movement for the bearer who, it is true, is already of noble blood, but who is clearly regarded as a member of an inferior caste. This makes it very similar to Celadon's previous disguise as "Lucinde." On both occasions, the disguise is taken at the behest of Adamas, the chief druid who elsewhere is quite conscious of Celadon's lower social status (I, 368). Social mobility, unacceptable to Adamas in life, lends an element of elasticity to the process of disguise, and separates it ostensibly from the sociopolitical realities of pastoral life, in a sense; from quite another perspective, we shall see later how the disguise of a whole class of "noble" shepherds provides the arena where sociopolitical tensions are worked out to a positive solution.

In the preceding cases, we can point to a trend in the chronological development of the disguise motif. Used initially in innocence, the mask tends to become entangled in moral and social concerns. What starts as a game or a device of romantic interest, ends up causing problems. This scenario is borne out in some individual instances of disguise, and it is seen in the overall development of the motif of disguise as the text progresses.

The last of the transsexual disguises continues the trend. In this instance, Ligdamon and Amerine (willy-nilly, husband and wife) exchange clothes and identities after Ligdamon has wounded a "knight" (Melandre, the woman disguised, IV, 769) in single combat. After leaving this "knight" wounded on the road, Ligdamon and Amerine effect the disguise to enable Ligdamon to escape recognition and prosecution for his act (IV, 690 ff.). The exchange of identity is prompted by Amerine, but is readily accepted by Ligdamon who is, by all accounts, a chivalrous knight in good standing.

The disguise is of interest to us because it is indicative of a breakdown in the code of chivalry. Prior to disguising as his wife, Ligdamon leaves his gravely wounded opponent to die on the road. To compound the gravity of this act, he hides behind his wife's identity to avoid responsibility for it. Such conduct would seem characteristically opposed to the canons of knightly conduct which direct the positive thematic forces. Nonetheless, Ligdamon (who himself narrates the episode) makes no effort to justify or apologize for so glaring a wrong.

Ligdamon makes no moral assessment of his actions, and neither does the text — this in spite of the fact that those actions are clearly of a questionable nature. Transsexual disguise again divorces itself from the service of love, in particular, and from the service of the most laudable ends, in general. At a point late in the text in the middle of political and social entanglements, disguise across sexual lines has ceased to be a toy in the hands of the innocent, and has become tainted with one degree or another of guilt or complexity. Through it, characters who stand as heroes may engage in conduct which is scarcely heroic; it may thus signal to us that characters' appearances may be deceiving, not only as concerns visible markers of identity, but also as concerns moral makeup as well.

Some general observations about *travestissement* in this romance are in order. One is that the morality of this type of disguise is most often glossed over by whichever narrator is speaking. In the case of the master narrator, the moral propriety of transsexual disguise is never called into question; for this narrator, the issue is morally inert. From an objective point of view, a moral progression from innocence to complication can be traced over the course of this disguise in *L'Astrée*. But the narrator's silence on this indicates a brand of moral relativism that preempts even the intransigent heroic code. Evidently, the ends of disguise serve to justify or condemn the means of disguise; it is not the disguise itself, with its attendant social and sexual overtones, which does so. In passing, we point to this dichotomy of intransigence and relativism as corroboration of Clifton Cherpack's argument that *L'Astrée* should not be taken for a properly philosophical document.[3]

A second observation is that the repeated incidence of transsexual disguise in this as in other pastorals, focuses attention on the matter of sexual identity — what it means to be a woman or man. Occasionally (as with Filidas) transsexual disguise comes into conflict with sexual identity; when this happens, the text draws on an implicit moral imperative to respect the "être," the inner reality. And yet, the same imperative does not bind, for example, with sociopolitical identity in a community where nobles receive the gods' blessing as they abdicate their rank and become shepherds.

When sexual identity does revolt against the mask, it shows the general instability of disguise — that disguise is, at its best, a temporary and topical solution which awaits a more permanent definition that is not based on illusion. Celadon's disguise as Alexis enjoys early success and effectiveness, but it becomes awkward to the point where his sexuality, at last defined, erupts and demands recognition. Similar tension is borne out on the level of society, where the noble ancestry of shepherds rises to the political and martial challenge when the "real" world encroaches upon their idyllic retreat (IV, 714 ff.).

Concerning sexual identity as it begins to emerge from our study of transsexual disguise, the matter of natural lots comes to the fore.

---

[3] Clifton Cherpack, "Form and Ideas in *L'Astrée*," *Studies in Philology* 69.3 (July 1972) 320-333.

To males befalls the responsibility to pursue in matters of love (this is why most disguises are assumed, for the men's part); to women befalls the charge to defend — either themselves or their loved ones; men are called upon by the pastoral ethic to be active, hence their sensitivity to political duty when it arises; the passivity which the pastoral ethic forces upon women leads them either to a preoccupation with moral honor and respectability, or to revolt against social values. The curious thing is that, for d'Urfé, this amounts to a thematic self-contradiction: the political system which governs the Forez is a matriarchy, where Queen Amasis is sovereign, and where nymphs constitute the ruling aristocracy; the same point holds for the religious tradition ascribed to the Forez society, namely, the religion of the druids which was historically a matriarchal institution.[4] So this could be a case in which seventeenth-century values come into conflict with the fictive fifth-century Gaul portrayed in the text; we shall see other examples of this sort of superimposition of values.

A third general point to be made, and an obvious one, is that the society of *L'Astrée*, as a matter of generic convention, is basically blind in a physical sense to changes of identity. The process of identification does not root itself in the visual, but rather directs the question of identity to issues of affiliations, beliefs, pursuits, deeds, and the like. Visual recognition is all but supplanted by the spoken word. The domain of appearances in the pastoral genre, the "paraître," takes control of the visual senses and establishes a rather unreliable identity as a function of conduct, association, and so on. In the domain of the reality underlying these appearances, the "être," identity is much more closely related to heritage (for example, ancestry, blood, etc.) than to mutable markers like physical aspect or name. Incapable of perceiving the physical disguise, a textual society in the tradition of pastoral romance must rely on its observation of what a character does and says outwardly in order to form its most dependable impression of what that character is. Hence the broad spectrum of illusion in character identity and the ease with which disguises work in the narrative.

Let us turn now to the other physical disguises put to use in the pastoral, to see what tendencies arise in the other facets of the mask motif.

---

[4] See Joseph Campbell, *The Masks of God: Occidental Mythology* (New York: Viking, 1976) 36.

4. The Other Physical Disguises

Social status is a medium of disguise in the same way that gender is: the appropriate clothes and conduct are donned in order to project a convincing illusion. Such a procedure could only be effective under the conditions that, first, the society in question be susceptible to trickery in the process of physical recognition and, second, the society be stratified to the degree that a disguise across its internal boundaries would create an illusion powerful enough to render true identity invisible. Both of these conditions obtain in *L'Astrée*, as Jacques Ehrmann makes the point emphatically:

> Si... les différentes classes se mêlent en principe, l'étanchéité entre chacune d'elles est finalement préservée malgré les incursions d'une classe à l'autre. En fait, les emprunts, les passages, les déguisements ne sont que temporaires et chacun se retrouvera au rang auquel il appartient essentiellement. (89)

It is because of the fact that the reality of social class is immutable that the appearance of change may be so effective a disguise. This is why a later assertion of Ehrmann is slightly misleading when he says:

> Dès qu'il s'agit de la structure essentielle de la société, personne ne se trompe. Chacun a parfaitement conscience de sa classe et de celle de son interlocuteur, même déguisé. (90)

The fact is that illusion is made to play on questions of identity as pertains to social class, and it is quite capable of clouding the "être" sufficiently to cause a degree of confusion, even if it never leads characters to question directly the fundamental social structure. The confusion of which we speak is semiological in that it arises from the absence of direct correlation between appearance and reality.

The social order itself is rather well defined in *L'Astrée*. At the top there is the ruling class consisting of Amasis, the queen nymph, Galathée (her daughter), Clidaman (her son), and the kings and princes of other lands who populate the narrative. The next stratum downward is occupied by the various "dames" and noblemen. Knights also partake of this noble status, but certain hints may be gleaned to the effect that they are considered more soldierly than lordly by the nymphs (see I, 330 and 338, for example). Separate from all these levels of nobility are the druids who, nonetheless, are treated with deference by all, and enjoy a degree of social nobility by virtue of their lofty position as intermediaries between gods and humans. In the case of Adamas, the chief druid, the issue is circumvented by the fact that he is blood-related to Amasis. He thus personifies the fusion of social and spiritual authority.

The society has other classes, specifically the soldiers and the servants. The soldiers' contact with the action is marginal, except for the fact that they represent a kind of blind, political force of strength in numbers. Servants, for the most part, are simple souls, being cast as the mere extension of their masters' values and ethics.

A low rung on the social ladder is held by the shepherd class, but their position here is somewhat curious. They are the rustic society, farthest from the court, the least "civilized" in the etymological sense of the term. And yet, much is made of their refined ways and of the fact that they have succeeded in bringing aristocratic comportment to the country. As a group, the shepherds of Forez are of a noble ancestry which sacrificed courtly life in exchange for divine protection. In so doing they brought about a doubling of the nobility and the creation of a new social class, a refinement of the social scheme which we shall elucidate at a later point.

We have already detected an evolution in the motif of disguise — from the idyllic to a nostalgia for the idyllic, from love to escape — and the same pattern will hold for disguises across lines of social class. Indeed, this pattern serves as a thematic guide for *L'Astrée* on the whole. The pastoral society is a utopian structure, but two independent sets of circumstances impede the realization of the ideal. First, the breakdown in reliable communication between lovers sets the society into turmoil from within. Second, the advent of "civilization," namely, the contact with the political realities which attend the noble class, threatens to topple the utopia from without. Left unhindered by these two factors, the shepherd society is self-sufficient and, ideally at least, optimally founded as a retreat from the harsh realities of the political world.

Yet it is through both the confusion in the semiotic system of love (i.e. that signs are misread between lovers) and the initiation to the sociopolitical facts of life in the "real world," that the pastoral society undergoes its rite of passage. It is shaken from the security of its optimal, innocent world, and forced to suffer the growing pains which comprise the collective "épreuve qualifiante" of the society. In this way, the society, nostalgic for the innocence of its youth, is compelled to look forward in anticipation to the restoration of a perfect social order. However, given the imposing political realities, the new utopia can only be instituted after that society has proven its mettle. What is sought is the innocence of the past, joined with the wisdom of experience (for the sake of restoring a reliable sign system in love) and the strength of maturity (for the sake of withstanding the pressures exerted by a corrupt society living at the borders of the shepherds' utopia).

Let us proceed then by examining sample cases of disguise involving social status.

The first such disguise in the text is the most interesting because of its uniqueness in involving a fundamental transgression. It is that of Climante who assumes the rank of druid in order to further the ends of the villain Polemas (I, 33 ff.). This is a disguise of rather long chronological standing in the text. Climante poses as a druid in order to arrange a rendezvous between Polemas and the nymph Galathée, and to persuade Galathée (via trickery) that Polemas is sent to her by supernatural powers. The scheme fails, since it is Celadon whom Galathée first sees at the designated place. Later in the romance (IV, 672 ff.), the disguise functions in Climante's attempts to secure Galathée's hand in marriage for Polemas; again Climante uses "artifice" and again he fails, since by this time the heroes are aware of his fakery.

The disguise fails to achieve its intended ends, but not because of any ability on the heroes' part to see through it. Instead, it is because Climante is overheard in his narration of his own actions (I, 156). Climante is first recognized as a fraud not because of ineffective disguise but because he is indiscreet. But once his treachery is unmasked, Climante retains some force, so great is the power of illusion in the pastoral:

Leonide et Silvie sçavoient assez que cet homme estoit un imposteur, mais elles ne laissoient d'en avoir frayeur, ayant opinion que ce qu'il faisoit sous le voile de la pieté et saincteté n'estoit que des oeuvres de sortilege et de magie, ce qui leur donnoit encore plus de frayeur et de terreur. (IV, 656)

Climante has something else besides his disguise on which to rely: he attempts, one might say, to use the social order against itself. Of course, a text so conscious and respectful of hierarchies in nature as *L'Astrée* could scarcely be expected to favor upward social movement via disguise on the part of an antagonist. Climante provides the only detailed case of such social movement in this romance.[1] It is obvious from the start that the text will not challenge the social order by calling the immutability of its hierarchy into question through the actions of a villain. Such questions are raised subtly and treated seriously through the actions of heroic characters.

That Climante has transgressed a natural hierarchy is never in doubt. What is never made explicit, however, is whether the principal offense is of a spiritual or social nature. Undoubtedly it is safe for us to assume that the two go together in this case, and are of equal gravity. Adamas, the chief druid, says of Climante:

...s'il y avoit moyen de l'attraper, je luy ferois bien payer avec usure le faux tiltre qu'il s'est usurpé de druyde. (I, 368)

But there is nothing to indicate the precise nature of Climante's guilt: Adamas reproaches the usurpation of a title, an outward sign. The underlying realities of religious genuineness and social class are grouped together under this outward sign of "tiltre" which, according to Adamas, Climante has violated. The offense on the level of "paraître" is perceived as such by the most important moral spokesman for the society.

This is the text's only clear-cut example of upward social movement in disguise, and it is linked with evil. This judgment is rendered verbally by several of the text's heroes, most notably Celadon (I, 381 and 386). Disguise of social status remains as potent an illusion as any, but its use is restricted to bar any effort to violate the

---

[1] We will not consider here the case of Celadon who masquerades as a "druide" and as a nymph, because his status is problematic — he is not considered a noble, yet much is made of his lofty ancestry (I, 368, for example). The nobility of the shepherd class will be treated later.

social order from the bottom upward. Society guards privilege jealously.

Next is an ordinary case of disguise of social standing. Lindamor, whom all believe to be dead after combat with Polemas, returns disguised as a gardener to work at the residence of his beloved Galathée (I, 357 ff.). This is much more what one would expect from a disguise across social lines: it involves downward social movement, it serves the ends of proper love, and the illusion of a new identity is created by physical disguise. Ordinary as it is it offers points of interest.

First, unlike most other disguises in *L'Astrée*, this one serves more than one purpose. Lindamor uses it to further his favor with Galathée, but he acts the part of a ridiculous bumpkin both to intensify the disguise and to produce a comic effect among the nymphs. Leonide, the secondary narrator, is also quite explicit in pointing out the linguistic element of the disguise: Lindamor need have no fear of visual recognition, but since the pastoral society hears better than it sees (as a matter of generic convention), he must avoid recognition of language. It is, as Leonide states, because

> ...il craignoit que ce qui avoit esté couvert par les habits ne fust descouvert par la parole. (I, 358)

This is indicative of a society whose perception is much more closely attuned to language than to physical aspect, and in which language is a more reliable means of identification than visible appearance. This is true in spite of the fact that language is a system of signs which can be learned and therefore manipulated: language is more immediately perceptible than physical differentiation for a society of storytellers and rhetoricians. For this reason, disguise of speech is carried off with more difficulty than the disguise of the physical being.

A second point concerning this case is the social atmosphere in which it is to occur. For the duration of Lindamor's courtship of Galathée up to this point, the ostensible objection is that her suitor is of a lower class than she (I, 330). It is therefore of consequence that Lindamor predicate his disguise on the distinction of social status: the guise of social inferiority is the very vehicle by which he overcomes the social inferiority separating him from Galathée. Thus the mask exploits its ironic possibilities since there is truly more to it than meets the eye.

But the scene, as well as the social question, soon becomes more complicated. It is into this situation that Celadon is introduced, and the nymph Galathée finds herself infatuated with the shepherd. In the two contiguous episodes we observe the following sequence of events: a nobleman (Lindamor) disguises as a peasant to win the affection of Galathée, over the mild objection of social inequality; he is subsequently supplanted in Galathée's favor by Celadon, a noble "disguised" as a shepherd. The nymph's nascent affection for Celadon prompts her to abandon her social rigor and to seek justification of her new love. In the latter case, however, the resounding objections of social inequality prevail, since Galathée is finally persuaded (albeit reluctantly) to sacrifice Celadon and to direct a more proper attention to Lindamor. The issue of social status permeates all of the princess' romantic entanglements, and her decisions thereupon stem either from the illusions of disguise or from concerns of social protocol.

The ensuing disguise of social rank involves one Arimant and his servant, Bellaris. Arimant disguises himself as his servant in order to escape from prison (III, 446 ff.). The means of this disguise are physical, but it is admitted in the narration that this one is weak: Arimant is able to escape in spite of the fact that "il luy ressembloit fort mal,... il estoit impossible de prendre l'un pour l'autre, pour peu qu'on y prit garde" (III, 447). We are told that Arimant escapes with ease because the order has been given to allow Bellaris to leave, and the guards "n'y regarderent de plus pres."

The failure of the eyes to recognize identity consistently underscores the fact that society is not beholden to the physical realm to any appreciable degree. Rather it is attuned to the realm of ideas and ideals, sensitive to signs of symbolic order, especially language. Nonetheless, the needs which prompt Arimant's disguise are quite pragmatic and far-removed from the ideal. So we see again what we observed in the case of transsexual disguise: in the latter parts of the romance, escape replaces love as the motivation for disguise.

Last among the disguises of social rank is that of the nymph Leonide who dons the garb of a peasant. She does so uniquely to escape the soldiers of Polemas who seek to abduct her (IV, 724 ff.). As was the case with disguises across sexual lines, the disguise across lines of social rank begins to raise ethical questions in the later stages of the text, engaging the motif of the mask in the same political and moral realities with which the society finds itself preoccupied.

The question here posed has to do with the plight of the inferior social classes: in her flight, Leonide accepts the hospitality of an old peasant woman (who disguises Leonide as a peasant); the nymph eludes soldiers who then burn down the old woman's house; Leonide, who leaves the woman to her own resources, sees the flames and vows to repay her for her loss, but no further mention is made of the issue. Even though we assume that a nymph's word is good, the action leaves the matter of social responsibility unresolved.

The social question goes further. The text's master narrator who relates this episode has several comments to make about the disguise as such, none of which is favorable to the lower social stratum. Says the narrator of Leonide-disguised: "...elle eust plutost fait rire, qu'elle n'eust donné de l'amour" (IV, 724), setting up an implicit and questionable opposition of loveliness and nobility versus laughability and low status. The nature of disguise is then commented upon overtly by Leonide when the *huissier* fails to recognize her true identity: "...ne cognoissez-vous les personnes qu'à l'habit?" (IV, 728), calling direct attention to the disparity between appearances and reality which is inherent in the mask. The motif is one in which *mérite* is supposed to shine through outer appearances and be recognized, but clearly the action of the entire romance belies this motif, as time and again the pastoral society wants to give outward appearances more credence and significance than they deserve.

This is the only case in the text where a nymph, of the highest social order, disguises downward socially. Sight of this disguise causes confusion among the noble peers of Leonide who express shock at the presence of a peasant, such presence being offensive to the nobility. And as was the case with Fleurial the gardener (IV, 727), the nymphs fail to recognize Leonide's face, but do identify her by voice (IV, 728).

The blindness of the society to physical disguise is shared by the nobility. But above all, the society is not blind to social distinction, and neither is the narrator who refers somewhat condescendingly to the garb of peasantry as "meschans habits," and sarcastically to Leonide as "bien parée" in "ses beaux habits" (IV, 729). Leonide herself is no different, expressing great shame for the appearance which actually saved her life (IV, 729).

Our study of the individual disguises across social lines has lent some insights into the dynamics of disguise in general. Aside from merely advancing the action (as does any such theatrical sort of motif), the disguise of social rank serves to bolster the text's social hierarchy — an order that remains fundamentally unchallenged in spite of game-playing which goes on around it. The disguise enables characters and narrator(s) alike to make comments, both explicit and implicit, about the nature of that social order. This type of disguise also informs the reader of the immutability of hierarchy, a fact which helps account for the effectiveness of the mask: it is so viable a mask, in part, because no one in the text can accept (and therefore cannot expect) any degree of social change.

Concerning the motivation for disguise of social status, we noted the same progression found in transsexual disguise. This is a passage from proper love, towards escape from the intolerable. As the society comes to terms with the realities that threaten it, a mechanism of escape must be found: in psychological terms it may be stated that a game must be introduced into the society's trials, in order for that society to maintain sight of its utopian goals. But this spirit of idealism does not obviate the responsibility to accept reality. In this the society does not fail, given the lesser frequency of disguises in the text's latter parts.

Under the general rubric of unilateral physical disguises — the assumption of new identity by one character — there remain only three cases of inert and thematically insignificant nature, and they need not be treated here. To proceed, then, we turn to those physical disguises in which a preexisting identity is assumed. In these, no new identity is forged. Where the previous cases turned on the ignorance of those whom the disguise was intended to deceive, the coming cases of identity exchange (and identity "theft") seek to play upon the knowledge of others, thus causing one character to be taken for another whose identity is already known. These disguises are three in number.

First among them is one which is interesting in that it involves a substitution of identity, not by the disguise of the character's person, but still by physical means. This is the case of Madonte who, at the behest of her servant Leriane, and in order to effect a retreat from courtly life, allows another young woman to receive visitors in her stead. The identity switch is made in the darkness of Madonte's chamber. The situation is complicated by the machinations of the perfidious Leriane who puts in Madonte's place a woman about to give birth. This causes all at court to assume that Madonte has had an illegitimate child (II, 245 ff.).

For Madonte, the disguise is successful, but she is unaware of its full scope. It remains in effect until the surrogate is persuaded to confess (II, 259). What is distinctive about it is that there is a third party who is apart from the actual process of disguise, but who is also its engineer and is the only character to see through it. A framed structure of illusion comes before us, in which the actors in one situation of disguise are themselves the victims of another level of illusion on which they are unwittingly functioning.

There is, then, a new type of character in the arena of disguise: the "ingenue" who is at the same time participant in, and victim of, her own freely accepted disguise. Through the plotting of a third party, Madonte is here led to precipitate her own downfall by permitting an identity exchange whose fullness she is not perceptive enough to grasp. This is the first instance we have seen of such irony (i.e. a deeper meaning unknown to a participating character) within the disguise motif.

The second identity exchange is the only one to be carried out between two lovers. Astrée and Celadon/Alexis don each other's garb, and it is one of the odder cases of disguise in the entire romance. The fact is that this is the only substitution of identity between lovers is noteworthy in light of Silvandre's doctrine (and the text's ostensible doctrine as well) which preaches that the lover ideally seeks to fuse his being with that of the beloved — in that sense, to "become" the beloved. Yet this is the sole instance in which a lover avails himself of disguise in order to accomplish this ideal on the level of illusion.

For Celadon, this disguise occurs within the context of another disguise, since it is with the "feinte druide" Alexis that Astrée swaps clothing. The inherent confusion in this framing process is made explicit by the narrator who speaks of "l'impatiente amour d'Alexis" (III, 592) instead of that of Celadon. This new disguise itself begins in an "illusion": Celadon/Alexis mistakenly puts on the robe of Astrée instead of his own. Then in a flight of affection he dons the rest of her outfit seeking some sort of metonymic expression for his love. But the illusion becomes real enough for the bearer:

> ...luy semblant que le bon-heur de toucher cette robbe qui souloit estre sur le corps de sa belle maitresse, ne se pouvoit egaler. (III, 596)

Unable to realize his amorous inclinations in reality, Celadon opts for the realm of illusion — specifically the realm of disguise. Illusion is the only possible reality in the idealized world which the pastoral society has created for itself.

After it is discovered that Alexis has taken the garb of Astrée, the women discuss how Astrée can complete an identity switch and, at the prompting of the nymph Leonide, Astrée agrees (III, 597). This points to another distinctive aspect of the case: it is the only disguise in the text that has no initial motivation other than sport (excluding Celadon's romantic impulses). The women contrive the disguise for no purpose other than to confuse the rest of the group and to enjoy themselves doing it.

However, the disguise occurs in two phases, creating a microcosm for the text's thematic plan and for the motif of disguise as well. If the disguise begins in the carefree atmosphere of play, it soon takes on a much more serious aspect in the context of the crisis which confronts society. Astrée, dressed as Alexis, is taken for the latter by Polemas' henchmen who seek revenge on Adamas, father of the real Alexis. Celadon rushes to the abductors' camp claiming to be the real Alexis (IV, 750). What this illustrates is again the passage from innocence to commitment which the society is forced to undergo in its quest for the reinstatement of the ideal order. Celadon may no longer stand by, playing the innocent game of disguise; however, in his commitment he avails himself of the weapon which has the greatest force for him, namely, disguise.

Disguise also shows here its metonymic effect. Where disguise is in essence a metaphorical event, a substitution based on resemblance, the mask itself (as a physical phenomenon) has a property of association by contiguity as well. Celadon experiences some degree of contact with his beloved by putting on her robe — and along with it, her identity. The illusion is real enough for him since the mask is authentic, by virtue of its past proximity to the woman he loves. In this theater of illusion, the prop of the mask now has thematic significance in its own right, endowed with the power to make illusions real for the player who wears it. Elsewhere in the pastoral, the mask itself, the physical medium of disguise, does not enjoy such an investment of meaning.

Last among the exchanges of identity is the case of Leonide who, while dressed as Galathée, is accidentally kidnapped by Polemas who mistakes her for the royal nymph (IV, 713 ff.). This disguise of the nymph Leonide is one of the very few in *L'Astrée* which has no previously stated intention; but it becomes clear to the reader that it is designed to protect the person of Galathée and to allow the antagonists to play out their hand. To this end the disguise is effective.

The narrator reports that a veil keeps Leonide's true identity from Polemas. Nonetheless, it is her voice which gives her away, and not the removal of a veil or the recognition of some visible trait. The spoken word again shows substance in the sphere of identity and remembrance.

The corpus of disguises in the exchange of identities is too limited for us to speak of a trend or a progression within it. Instead we may see in it the further variation of the mask, which here displaces the identity of the person in question rather than hiding it. The disguise also shows us its sport, the game which is at last recognized as such, so played by the characters.

There remains only one variety of physical disguise for our study: that of the total withholding of identity by physical means. This type does not create a new identity for character, nor does it substitute a preexisting one. Rather, it functions as the complete mask, serving to hide all identity and not to deceive further. The disguises which fall into this category are not as complex as those already seen, since the identification process is merely stopped, and not misled by false appearances. With the mask of anonymity, the identity of character remains a mystery to other characters and even, at times, to the reader. We shall examine only one such case here, the other two (Lindamor I, 345, and Damon II, 257, ff.) being rather straightforward and contributing little to the development of the motif.

Very early in the text, as the second of all disguises recounted in *L'Astrée*, is found the story of Alcippe, the father of Celadon, and of a woman of rank who was in love with him. This inserted narrative is set a generation prior to the rest of the action in the text. For obvious social reasons, the woman keeps her identity secret for the duration of her affair with Alcippe who is brought blindfolded to her each night. They meet only in total darkness. The secondary narrator of the tale (Celadon) refers to the woman only as "la dame incognue" and never divulges her identity. For Alcippe's part, he is finally able to guess the woman's identity by cutting off a piece of her linen in the darkness, and comparing the livery the next day (I, 57-59). Upon hearing herself named in the darkness, the woman terminates the affair thus making the integrity of her disguise the *sine qua non* of her romantic involvement with Alcippe. The reader is told that Alcippe has gone to his grave without revealing the noble woman's identity to a soul.

The love affair represents a double transgression for Alcippe: first, the woman is of a higher social rank than he; second, he has already pledged his love to the shepherdess Amarillis, whom he eventually marries. Therefore, the disguise of the "dame incognue" plays a key role in the narrative, aside from merely heightening the mystique: it precludes any personal involvement in the affair on Alcippe's part, and thus it acts as a buffer for him against transgression of the masculine code of love (fidelity, service, submission to the will of the beloved, etc.); as a consequence, the affair remains solely on the physical level for Alcippe, a far cry from the ostensible neoplatonic "thesis" of this romance.

For the woman, the disguise of darkness provides total anonymity without the substitution of false identity. As a disguise, it is unique in the text in that the woman is the only truly important character who is deprived of nominal identity. Anonymity provides a depth of character for this mysterious figure: she is the only character in *L'Astrée* whose sole identity is her disguise, and who functions as a personification of the motif.

At this point, we have concluded our census of physical disguises in *L'Astrée*. But before going on to draw general conclusions on the motif of the mask, we shall pause only briefly to consider a subject which, in the pastoral tradition with all its theorizing and polemics on love, deserves to be considered a form of disguise. This is the illusion in behavior which is consistently taken by society for a change in the nature of a character, tantamount to a change in identity, namely, feigned love.

5. Behavioral Disguises

We turn to a variety of disguise which does not mask the character in the traditionally understood sense, but rather seeks to alter the opinion which society has of him — the opinion of the nature and conduct by which the pastoral society may identify him. To the end of changing this set of outwardly perceived markers, the character engages in feigned conduct; in the pastoral tradition, the only feigned conduct of any importance to the system of character identification is feigned love. This behavioral mask plays not on the unreliable vision of those deceived, but on their knowledge of the disguise-bearer's past conduct, and on the contrast between the past and the character's present behavior.

Throughout the history of pastoral literature, a character's identity and his or her relation to society is forged upon that character's past. He or she is known to others, and judged by them, with respect to the past. The tradition of such characterization is respected by d'Urfé who takes his cue directly from Montemayor in the portrayal of characters faithful to the heroic code. Celadon, Astrée, and a host of others take from d'Urfé's hand the characteristics of the faithful lovers, since, in description and portraiture, almost everything relating to them in the narrative pertains to this trait.

Indeed, Celadon's story is the tale of his affection for Astrée: one knows practically nothing else about his personal past (except his lineage, which is important), aside from the fact that he has always been in love with Astrée; this is his past and as such it defines his present — all that he is in the present. Hence it forms a great part of his identity. Likewise, Hylas' story — that which he himself narrates when asked to fill the others in on his past — is largely the saga of his actual or attempted amorous conquests. True to the customary situation in the text, Hylas' past defines his present and thus his identity in the society. He is, after all, known to one and all as the inconstant lover. His past (I, 294-309 and III, 350-364) constitutes the identity by which he is known to society and reader alike. For either of these characters to change his values in the sight of society — to subscribe outwardly to a new code of love — would be like changing his name or his family. Society would simply not identify him in the same way any longer.

Silvandre provides an interesting case. Throughout *L'Astrée*, one learns very little of his past, the past of which he himself is ignorant. With his ancestry and early youth unknown, he has only his formal education and his philosophies upon which to base his social being. Consequently, and in lieu of any other tradition, he creates for himself the tradition of the philosopher and propagandist of constancy in love. By these signs he is known to all, therefore they create the only real identity he has, even though the text paves the way for his eventual recognition as the true son of Adamas.

Since characters tell untiringly their love stories and their beliefs on the issues of love, we must conclude that love constitutes an important segment of a character's identity (as in fact it does in all the pastoral tradition). It follows from the fact that, if textual figures may be identified by their love, an attempt to project an illusion in love (and thereby falsify this identity) may constitute a disguise. So how is it, one may ask, that of the types of behavioral illusions seen in the text, we consider as disguise only feigned love?

This question may be answered in two ways. First, the reader (especially one familiar with the pastoral tradition since antiquity) soon recognizes in *L'Astrée* that love is the one form of behavior sufficiently dynamic and universal to provide identity markers for characters. All textual figures of any thematic import (except the two presiding ones, Amasis and Adamas) may be identified by their singular romantic inclinations; Hylas is identified mainly by his wandering amorous tendencies; likewise, the few lovers in the text who prove unfaithful stand out by virtue of this trait. Love and the way a character loves give information about the character. How a character's conduct in love relates to the accepted code gives others a way to categorize him or her. Love thus can provide a label, a form of identity useful in differentiating one character from another: all characters have the same range of emotions, almost all men are courageous and show great prowess in battle, almost all female characters show the same value system and conduct, and of course all textual figures speak in the identical articulate and lyrical precious style. The only type of outward conduct which may differentiate one from another is the romantic: the one whom he or she loves, the manner of this love, the degree of fidelity, and the effects of love upon the lover as situations change. The handful of antagonists (themselves also lovers) are the only ones who enjoy any kind of singularity of conduct aside from the romantic; however, this distinction is only by character type. We find, on the other hand, that subtlety in *behavioral* identity is a function of love. Since love alone serves as such an identifying process, its falsification must be considered as a disguise.

Similarly, we may also say that illusion in love is the only type of conduct which poses the problem of the mask: only feigned love is capable of creating confusion between illusion and reality, even among lovers and perpetrators of the illusions, raising doubts that go straight to the inner being of character — and, thereby, touching on issues of identity. As a behavioral illusion which seeks to change the outward impression emanating from the heart of the inner self, feigned love stands alone as a disguise. In no sphere of activity other than the romantic is there a behavioral illusion which qualifies as a disguise according to our standards: the recognition relationship between appearance and essence is not tested by conduct (except in love) as it is by physical disguise. Even the consummate impostor, Climante, bases his illusions upon physical disguise of his true identity.

With all this in mind, we proceed with our consideration of the behavioral mask. There are ten instances of this in the text.[1] The point will be quite clear enough if we pause to consider only the first two.

The very first of all illusions in *L'Astrée* — a text whose action and thematic strategy are, in large part, predicated upon illusion — is a disguise whose medium of illusion is behavior. The first mask in a text that abounds in masks, its proximity to the beginning of the romance sets the tone for this essential thematic aspect. It provides

---

[1] See this author's doctoral dissertation, "The Character Under the Mask: Disguise and Identity in *L'Astrée*," diss., University of Pennsylvania, 1980, 94-110, for a detailed survey of these ten cases and the other disguises which are not treated in the present study.

the situation for the narrative's *in medias res* beginning. This mask of Celadon is responsible for his predicament throughout the rest of the narrative and therefore sets the direction for most of his actions. It establishes this character as one whose principal reliance is upon illusion, since the reader first sees him engaged in this sort of disguise; subsequent disguises in the narrative which we have already considered serve to confirm this typology. And it shows that disguise, as the text's beginning, will be more than a motif in that it provides from the outset much of the stuff of narrative in *L'Astrée*.

It is agreed between Astrée and Celadon that, in order to divert attention from their relationship, he will feign love for Aminthe (I, 10 ff.). The idea is that of Astrée, and Celadon accepts only reluctantly: the disguise is at first carried out with difficulty even though Celadon will, throughout the narrative, come to be known by his involvement with disguise. In any event, the plan goes awry through the treachery of Semire who plays on Astrée's latent jealousy, and convinces her that Celadon's affection for Aminthe is genuine. This misinterpretation on the part of Astrée, of the illusion which she herself perpetrated, causes Celadon's first banishment and his attempted suicide. He spends the greater part of the remainder of the text trying to undo the effects of this disguise which goes wrong.

This first of the text's disguises illustrates much of the dynamism of the motif of illusion in general. It likewise, and more importantly, serves as a model for disguise: early on it meets with success, but later it encounters complications which render it quite problematic for the participants. The source of difficulty is the inability of Astrée to distinguish "fact" from her own fiction; this situation points at once to the availability and to the potency of disguise, for, at a given moment, any character can be the perpetrator and victim of a mask — even of one and the same mask. Each character can initiate as well as fall prey to an illusion, since each possesses the faculty of deception and the faulty perception which make illusion possible.

The ostensible objective of the disguise is the furtherance of love through the illusion of a different situation. The charade, we are told (I, 19), is particularly onerous for Celadon, the mask-bearer for whom the conflict of disguise is narrated in terms which involve the very essence and the basic identity of the character; he has said: "que... vous me commandiez de mourir, et non point de servir, comme que ce soit, autre qu'Astrée" (I, 19). Celadon is, of course, faithful beneath the mask, but the mask is taken by others for reality, and to such a degree that it obscures reality. Like the "fontaine de la Verité d'amour" whose conveyance of meaning (in its function as a sign) is interrupted, so too this disguise of Celadon causes an interruption in the identifying passage from appearance to reality, from "paraître" to "être." Since the society can no longer count on the simple correlation of appearance and reality, the combination of illusion and inaccurate perception is sufficient to call identity into question.

Once the disguise is introduced, the signifier no longer points reliably to the signified, hence the name "Celadon" is no longer, in the vision of Astrée, the sign of the faithful lover, and therefore the character has lost a measure of his identity. In order for him to regain it, he must conquer his own illusion: consequently, for Celadon, the text is spent in quest of that identity and in reinstating the reliability of the sign. Time and again his main weapon in this struggle is that which initially caused his troubles: disguise.

This is, naturally, one of the great paradoxes of *L'Astrée*: why does Celadon persist in his disguising? His masks do not regain either his identity or the reliability of the sign. On the contrary, one may say that the text cannot end as long as Celadon errs in this quest by using disguises, and, in so doing, by continuing the semiotic malaise. It seems that, in the complex network set up for codified communication in the pastoral society, truth must first be translated into illusion in order to be understood, and identity must be proven by disguise for the character-in-quest to resume a normal life.

The second behavioral disguise in the text involves another of the ostensible paragons of proper love. Lycidas, the brother of Celadon, is in love with Phillis; in order to hide this affair, Phillis and Astrée invent the ruse by which Lycidas feigns affection for Olimpe, a shepherdess who has come to visit (I, 134 ff.). Olimpe is characterized as vain, and she becomes the first victim of the disguise in assuming that Lycidas is genuine in his courtship of her. We are told explicitly (I, 135) that Olimpe plays more the seeker than the sought after — something of a sexual role-reversal which is not uncommon in *L'Astrée* — and in so doing she manages to move the feelings of Lycidas. This is the same Lycidas who has early and often protested his fidelity and love for Phillis.

The victimization of Olimpe has its origin in a faulty perception — indeed in a habit of faulty perception on her part: "...il luy sembloit que tous les bergers qui la regardoient, en estoient amoureux..."

(I, 134). Her susceptibility to outward signs leads directly to her inability to see through the mask which is assumed by Lycidas; in this she differs from other characters whose deficient perception is a shared trait of nature, since hers is specifically attributed to her personality. This sets her somewhat apart from the others: in her case, gullibility is motivated, whereas in the others it appears to be inherent.

As regards Lycidas, this disguise is something of an anomaly for the reader. Elsewhere in the text there is no sign that Lycidas' love for Phillis is anything less than exemplary, and yet, conspicuous by their absence are the impassioned protests against the imposed mask of feigned love. This indication is borne out by subsequent events, for the secondary narrator (Astrée) states outright that "la feinte en fin fut à bon escient" (I, 135). The mask at least temporarily becomes real in a strange series of occurrences: "Lycidas (ayant eu d'elle tout ce qu'il en pouvoit avoir)" (I, 135) holds Olimpe in contempt, but not too much to prevent him from yielding to her advances, to the extent that she finally becomes pregnant. Interestingly, Lycidas reverses the mask as he comes to Astrée to complain of the initial disguise, and Astrée (only as narrator) realized the doubling of the mask: "... il me... vint raconter avec tant d'apparance de desplaisir..." (I, 135). Lycidas therefore has assumed a disguise which becomes genuine, necessitating a second disguise to cover the first, and which would seek to portray the original state of affairs. In the end, Lycidas repents and wishes to regain the favor of Phillis.

The text invokes its ready double-standard to extricate Lycidas from this predicament which, elsewhere in *L'Astrée*, would seem hopeless. Astrée, pleading the cause of Lycidas before Phillis and the reader, ascribes the indiscretion to the youthful weakness of the shepherd and, in a matter of a few sentences, is able to set him back in the good graces of Phillis. The incongruity with the text's ostensible thesis of proper love is quite obvious here, especially in light of so glaring an offense.

If this case seems incongruous considered alone, then the strangeness of the situation is only amplified by its juxtaposition with the first disguise of Celadon, the narration of which precedes it almost immediately. Lycidas is lightheartedly forgiven for the offense of which Celadon is merely suspected; the judgment against Celadon, however, drives him to attempted suicide. The contrasts between these two cases of illusion are contiguous in the general narrative: Celadon's goes awry, where that of Lycidas becomes all too perfectly borne; the innocent Celadon is condemned by Astrée who has already argued for the forgiveness of Lycidas, the guilty one.

Yet the two masks are donned initially for the identical purpose of diversion. One motivation generates two disguises which then follow radically differing courses, worn by two brothers, and coexisting almost side by side in the narration. This outlay of the submotif of behavioral disguise here sends an implicit message to the reader: the ostensible thesis of a text which puts forth such a blatant incongruity relating to that thesis, must be taken with a grain of salt; the didactic reading of *L'Astrée* as a document of neoplatonic codification of love is discounted by the oppositions between these cases of similar disguise.

In the aggregate, the cases of feigned love occurring in the text serve a variety of purposes, ranging from the didactic to the humorous, from entertainment to intrigue. A preponderance of negative overtones would seem to make a point about such conduct, given that many of these disguises end up confusing the very affairs which they set out to ameliorate. Feigned love can be too effective a disguise, giving rise to an illusion that goes out of control and becomes stronger even than its perpetrators. In other words, feigned affections prove to be at least as dangerous as the infidelities which sometimes accompany genuine affections. The illusion of love is declared a dangerous terrain in a land where true love is held to be a prime motivating force.

With the behavioral illusions we bring to a close our survey of the various types of play on the means of character identification.[2] A general conclusion on the matter of disguise would seem in order, and we proceed to this in the following chapter.

---

[2] Let us take this occasion to mention that the text also sets forth four instances of identities created or altered by a change in name only. The character Silvandre is the most notable example. Since this alteration of true identity is purely nominal and involves none of the other dynamics of disguise, it is not judged as calling for detailed study here. See this author's doctoral dissertation (note 1 above), pages 111 ff. for a survey of these nominal disguises.

6. General Inferences on Disguise

To arrive at a good understanding of the motif of disguise in *L'Astrée* is to keep critical sight of two things: d'Urfé's thematic debt to the long pastoral tradition, and the particular depth which he affords the motif. On the one hand, none of the *types* of disguise in d'Urfé's work represents an innovation; all are illustrated in his two principal models, the *Diana* and the *Arcadia*, and most can be seen in some form over and over in the pastoral dating from antiquity. On the other hand, d'Urfé makes new use of the motif in the frequency and force with which the mask comes into conflict with reality; while the tension between disguise and reality is not new to the pastoral (especially since Montemayor), d'Urfé's characters give nuance to it as their quest for reliable identity turns into a matter of continuing thematic concern.

Some unique circumstances obtain in *L'Astrée* to make so much of disguise. One is the fact that a main character in the central action, Celadon, has his identity and his actions engaged in disguise for virtually the whole text. But another special circumstance in this work has to do with an actual thematic of *truth* and how it pertains to the characters' use of illusion and to the system of character identification in general.

The various modes of disguise all meet with about the same degree of success in *L'Astrée*. One evident reason for this is that the society in the text is, in general, deprived of an objective criterion of truth. This applies, of course, not only to the sphere of identity, but to all facets of life. At every turn, important events and signs must be interpreted for the society by the voices of its deeper consciousness, the druids, who often admit to their own fallibility. In the political arena, deception is the order of the day. In matters of love, women are compelled as a matter of social custom to mistrust the affections of men. And nowhere is the lack of an objective criterion of truth more evident than in the fact that the society is without the use of the Fontaine de Verité d'Amour. This is the fountain whose reflection shows the face of the lover if his or her love is returned; but for almost the entire narrative, the use of this lone objective standard of truth is prohibited by a supernatural spell.

The secret of the fountain, the secret of love without illusion, is guarded by two enchanted lions, and remains effectively inaccessible behind a labyrinth of paths. This is, as Ehrmann is careful to point out, indicative of the difficulty involved in the society's search for truth.[1] The principal goal of the society being the realization of proper love, the fountain represents the only sure means to this end without illusion. Consequently, as long as the fountain is not at the disposal of this society, illusion will remain a part of love — which is tantamount to saying that illusion will remain a part of the very fiber of this society.

It is understandable that illusion becomes, paradoxically yet necessarily, a part of the search for truth. Pursuing truth in a world of illusion, the noble and the shepherd alike are constrained to live with that illusion and to use it to a loftier (and ultimately justifiable) end. In this way, disguise becomes the illusion created and destined to overcome illusion. The masking of essence is a necessary tool in this world, since all other tools fail or are taken away; if the mask is engaged in a justifiable cause, the means of illusion itself merit the approval of the spokesman for the heroic conscience.

In comparison to the rest of the pastoral tradition, *L'Astrée* lends its disguise motif a remarkable degree of fullness, frequency, and organization. At virtually every phase of the action a disguise appears as an indispensible means of advancement; all sorts of disguises appear in the text, organized as they are into a network covering the expanse of this enormous work. *L'Astrée* takes a traditional motif and refines it, developing it to a great level of richness and codification. This situation did not escape the attention of Bruce Morrissette:

> Un autre élément qui avait opéré dans les romans antérieurs à *L'Astrée* d'une façon plus ou moins mécanique, c'est le déguisement, qui trouve aussi dans l'oeuvre de d'Urfé son épanouissement et sa plénitude baroque. Le doublement et le dédoublement des êtres, les personnages ambigus, le travestissement, la feinte: tout y paraît dans un échange

---

[1] Ehrmann 73.

perpétuel d'identités qui fait de l'intrigue presque tout entière un système de personnalités fausses, un jeu de miroirs où les caractères se substituent les uns aux autres, pénétrant par le déguisement et la feinte dans les milieux défendus, triomphant de la réalité par l'illusion et le change.[2]

Our investigation of the disguises across sexual lines turned up several significant points, not the least of which is the fact that this category is numerically the largest of all those considered. This would indicate that transsexual disguise is the easiest, or at least the most efficient of all. It is likewise indicative of the fact that sexual identity is least well defined in the society (witness, for example, the thematic of androgyny) since it is the one form of identity which is most frequently played upon. Indeed, the establishment of sexual identity is the most troublesome for the members of this society.

The society is in a state of transition in several respects, including the definition of sexual identity. The young in the text are clearly involved in a passage from separate, homogeneous sexual environments to a heterogeneous one. In most cases, the relationship of proper love experienced by one of these characters is the first serious encounter with a member of the opposite sex: prior to this point, the young man remains in the company of young men, and likewise the young woman with young women. For each character, the love experience is a venture out of this homogeneous atmosphere, but the passage is never quite complete in our corpus of the text.

Consequently the young characters function more comfortably with members of their own sex, communicating in an open and relaxed manner. Such communication is impossible across sexual lines (as what appears to be a matter of social protocol and even generic convention). Instead, members of the same sex spend nights together, exchanging stories, clothes, and sometimes even identities, all under the encouragement of social priorities. This affinity is sometimes expressed in almost erotic terms when, for example, a woman may say that she would be attracted to a certain other woman were she herself a male, as does Fossinde (IV, 121). Even the great lover, Hylas, says at one point that he prefers his friend Periandre to any of the women (II, 172). And the druid Adamas feels compelled to apologize to foreigners for the homosexual overtones of the diversions of the shepherd society (III, 499).

---

[2] Bruce Morrissette, "Structures de sensibilité baroque dans le roman pré-classique," *Cahiers de l'Association Internationale des Etudes françaises* 11 (May 1959) 95.

It is from this situation that the characters are attempting to realign their sexual priorities and affinities. But it is at this juncture that problems — serious communication problems — come to the fore, for as we have observed, the road to the fulfillment of proper love cannot be without the obstacles of illusion and misinterpretation. Perhaps we have found a cause at the source of this difficulty. The passage from homogeneous environment to heterogeneous entails a necessary adjustment in interpersonal relationships since, up to this point, each sex has been a discrete and sequestered entity, independent of the other. Contact with the opposite sex thus requires the establishment of common denominators that heretofore have not existed, but must be found if the passage is to be made. And it is the venture in the direction of establishing these new links which causes the great problems at the outset of the text. Consider the case of Celadon who, having left the almost exclusive company of his brother, is attempting to produce a favorable setting for his new love affair with Astrée. His intentions are misread by her, and he is banished by Astrée who becomes decidedly antimasculine for most of the text's remainder. She finds solace only in returning to her previous circle of female friends, and Celadon can only regain admission to her presence by dressing as a female.

It is thus no great coincidence that Celadon is able to relate more openly and comfortably with Astrée from behind the transsexual mask. By "becoming" a woman, he obviates the necessity for establishing a new, untested means of communication with her. Since she is most comfortable in the company of women, his transsexual disguise renders him more compatible with her for the moment. This mechanism of illusion works with remarkable smoothness until the point when, on the one hand, Celadon is unable to be all that a woman must be, and on the other hand, his masculinity finally comes to rebel against the constraints of the mask.

A careful study of the submotif of transsexual disguise shows it often to be born of similar motives — the quest for communication between the sexes. At a loss for a means of heterosexual communication in a society which is organized to prevent it, characters often disguise as members of the opposite sex to take advantage of a preexisting affinity. Strong bonds are there for the taking, and consequently the transsexual disguise has a great prospect for success even before it is undertaken.

The advancement of love interest is not, of course, the only function served by the transsexual disguise. It also is a way of escape when the occasion requires. In such cases, the disguise functions in the usual way. But what is of interest here is again the notion of passage: in the same way that the society is in transition from homogeneous to heterogeneous groupings, it is also in the process of passing from the innocence of love to a point of political commitment — this in direct response to the pressures brought to bear on the society from without.

The great central disguise in this category, that of Celadon/Alexis, may be seen as a microcosm of the transsexual disguise in the text, and of the motif in general. At its inception the disguise renders the transition of male to female very smooth for Celadon: the mask is comfortably borne and meets with total success. But Celadon experiences increasing difficulty in this disguise and finds himself less and less able to suppress his true sexual identity. The evolution of transsexual disguise through the text pursues a similar course, beginning in ease and innocence, and ending in a confrontation with reality under more difficult circumstances. And the motif as a whole shows, if only through its numerical incidence in the text, that disguise serves often in the idyllic beginning, whereas it proves to be less frequently resorted to (and consequently, less effective) when the society is confronted with a difficult situation. The power of illusion diminishes as reality takes a grip on the pastoral world.

The breakdown of directions of disguise across sexual lines is as follows: five men disguise as women, five women disguise as men, and two cases of identity exchange involve couples. This traces a perfect symmetry, although Celadon himself accounts for three of the male-to-female guises. This tells us something about the character who spends the great part of his time in the text disguised as a woman: while the mask enables him to pursue his personal goals, it is also a means of escape for him — a sort of abdication of the responsibilities of virility. The other men who disguise as women do not do so to the same degree: they do not adopt the manners of women as Celadon does; in addition, the narrator often makes a point of stating how well Celadon plays the role and how feminine his face, his gestures, and even his voice are. Our explanation for Celadon's affinity to feminine identity is rooted in the fact that, as a character, he is in search of his identity, and included in this is the quest for his sexual identity.

As for the women who disguise as men, the mask is often accompanied by an assumption of the outward traits of masculinity. It suffices for a woman to adopt the clothing of a man or the armor of a knight for her to summon the physical strength (quite unseen in the pastoral setting) to compete in combat. The means by which women defeat men in combat are sometimes fortuitous, but the results are still the same: physical disguise can entail the transfer of attributes other than the external. This phenomenon tends to establish an equality between the sexes, since a masculine superiority of strength is neutralized by outward appearances; for the rest, Melandre is able to assume masculinity to the same degree that Celadon is able to assume femininity. In the end, it is clear that a barrier exists between the sexes — a gap of communication which must first be breached by means of disguise, appealing to (and because of) the sexually homogeneous nature of society, before communication between woman and man is possible. A pattern is suggested in the text whereby a character must first infiltrate the exclusive circle of the opposite sex under the guise of illusion, in order to develop and test the bonds of a more profound heterosexual relationship.

Transsexual disguise is not merely a physical phenomenon but a linguistic one as well. The master narrator participates in certain cases of disguise by referring to a disguised character in the grammatical modes appropriate for a member of the opposite sex. This added dimension contributes to the strength of the motif as a whole, underscoring the effectiveness of the power of illusion; however, it also hints at the inherent equality of the sexes since it posits as total those changes which are ostensibly only external.

Concerning the disguises that involve the appearance of change across lines of social distinction, we have seen that disguise serves to reinforce an already entrenched and, for the narrative's purposes, natural social order. The code of values is implicit, one of the fixity of hierarchy within the society: first and foremost, the society is theocentric, and divine authority is passed along a fixed chain of human command — disguise being the only way of effecting transgression of this order; the druids (especially Adamas) interpret and administer divine will as it is expressed in the oracles; the noble caste, with its own inner hierarchy, represents the political actualization of this authority, as well as the natural superiority which goes along with noble birth and conduct; the shepherd caste willingly accepts a low rung on the social ladder, showing deference to all others, yet exhibiting a level of cultural refinement befitting the nobility.

If the social structure were to remain there, one would have no complications to deal with, and there would be no surprises for the reader already familiar with the social priorities of the seventeenth century in France. But such is not the case. A certain confusion is built into the social structure by virtue of the fact that some of the shepherds (most notably Celadon) are of noble blood, their ancestors having retired from courtly life in favor of the rustic tranquility of shepherd life. In a very real sense, these characters have abdicated the responsibility of the noble caste which is to heed the call of their blood to lead the society, and to perform this function from a position of prominence. Thus their very existence as shepherds is a disguise across social lines: the essence of nobility in shepherds' garb.

This raises quite a point about the motif of disguise. We must interpret three important facts in light of this "nobility in disguise": first, that the affairs of the shepherds are eclipsed by those of the nobles as the text progresses; second, that the incidence of disguise in the text's first volume is great, while it is much less in any of the subsequent volumes; and third, that the rustic utopia is invaded by the reality of the political sphere in the latter half of the text. The point is that, since disguise becomes less effective and since the rustic life must sacrifice its innocence for commitment, the nobility in shepherds' clothing is experiencing a call to return, in a certain measure, to the reality of its true, former identity. To the extent that this is so, the true and original social order is shown a kind of nostalgic respect while a new, "acceptable" social class is created nonetheless.

Fantasy, escapism and disguise become less and less viable as the text goes on: they no longer suffice as a mode of life in response to a call to commitment. Of course, there are other factors in play here, other social questions which lend deeper meaning to this creation of a new social stratum and which we shall consider in the conclusion of this work. In any event, the concerns of the nobility come to occupy the most attention of the narrative, and the political imbroglio that accompanies the nobility is the heart of the action. Therefore it is impossible for a shepherd to live in peace, and more particularly, it becomes impossible for a noble to live simply and in tranquility as a shepherd.

The point is borne out symbolically by Celadon who finally rebels against the feminine mask in the fourth volume's great battle scene, and literally by Silvandre who discovers his true noble identity. These two metamorphoses are rites of passage in that they shed false identities in favor of underlying truth. Disguises in general must yield their importance as society is summoned back to reality — a reality which will cause each character to identify herself or himself in truth and to act according to that truth. Reality presents itself as we have noted, in the form of political crisis, so starkly that the narrator states explicitly of the countrysides:

> car eux qui n'estoient autrefois que les douces cachettes de quelques honnestes larcins d'amour, et qui n'avoient accoustumé que d'ouyr les ardantes plaintes, les petites quereles, et les agreables paix des amants, ou leurs amoureuses entreprises, estoient maintenant une retraite de voleurs, et de ravisseurs inhumains. (IV, 747)

We are told relatively early in the text that the nobles who abandoned the court in favor of the rustic life, did so in a pact with the gods whereby the gods would spare them from attack by an outside political force. The gods seem to go back on this contract because, it would seem, it is more important for the society to find its true identity and definition. Only then will it outgrow the need for illusion and disguise, having already arrived at an understanding and acceptance of its own identity.

In our survey of disguises, we included the phenomenon of feigned love because of the privileged status accorded love in the narrative and in society. A character being known as a function of how and whom he or she loves, any illusion in this area becomes a disguise. The survey of all such cases in the text points out the progression described above, that as political life becomes more problematic, so does the use of behavioral disguise.

In the main, the great majority of disguises serve only as a means (albeit indispensable) to an end. In a society where illusion is by default a necessary weapon, the characters do not often derive meaning from that illusion, preferring only to use disguise and not to study it. This is typical of the pastoral society which learns not through its eyes or other senses, but through its intuited principles (for example, in the areas of love, theology, ontology, etc.). Thus characters do not often bear disguise with the direct intention to find meaning, but rather they bear it with another fixed goal in mind, most often depriving the mask of an inherent significance or specific semiological value — Celadon chooses to mask as Alexis not because of what the real Alexis signifies, but because the mask is convenient; such is the case in most disguises.

This leads us to reiterate the observation that the pastoral society (and this is true for the entire pastoral tradition) is fundamentally blind to essence, seeing signs but not pondering the signification process.

The functioning of this society is not predicated upon visual recognition or verification. Indeed, visual recognition is consistently lacking or unreliable, therefore disguise is able to derive its great potency. And this in itself comes as no surprise, for the societies of the pastoral since antiquity are not primarily occupied with the physical plane of existence: sex is, with few exceptions, intellectualized, love is idealized, physical conditions (climate, terrain, etc.) are rarely of consequence. In *L'Astrée* as in most pastorals, the physical description of character is scarcely even undertaken. Therefore, the physical life of the society is reduced to two things in *L'Astrée*: combat and disguise. All the rest of existence is words, thoughts, and feelings.

Disguises, even those which are most deceptive, are sometimes seen through by characters who have been fooled by them up to that point. Invariably the veil of blindness to disguise is lifted from their eyes at a moment of crisis or great tension. This can be interpreted in two ways: undeniably it is a generic *topos*, since in a literature of disguise there will also be a motif of anagnorisis at key points, for the advancement of action; but it also shows that disguises crack under pressure, that while the society is itself fooled by them under normal conditions, the disguises are adversely affected by external circumstances.

Lastly, there are moral aspects of the question of disguise, in spite of the fact that inconsistencies are obvious. The mask does, in certain instances, present an occasion of "sin" to the bearer. The feigned love of Lycidas leads to an illegitimate pregnancy; Celadon and Hylas brave the law by entering the temple of women in their transsexual disguises; likewise Celadon's other transsexual disguises are the means by which he breaks the "laws" of either Galathée or Astrée. In all of these cases, the ethical issue is of importance since these are heroic or positive characters. Yet their transgressions are glossed over, while those of villainous characters are not.

The text exhibits a moral relativism which works to absolve the heroes of guilt in disguise. The villains are less lucky. In cases where the latter mask their identity, the full weight of the moral system falls inexorably upon them; heroes, on the other hand, are pardoned by society and (implicitly) by narrator alike. The glaring inconsistency points to a major means of identification in the romance: characters are first and foremost identified by type, for or against truth and good, heroic or villainous.

The text's moral system therefore counts heavily on the system of identification — a standard of identity which underlies disguise and, it is hoped, does not bend to it. A character is defined in general as good or bad, but only the reader and the perspicacious Adamas are privy for sure to this information. The fact that other characters do not have so reliable an aid in identification fosters the great success of disguise in *L'Astrée*. As for the characters on the side of good, there are two types of transgression: that which is justified by dictum (of Adamas, for example), and that which is simply ignored. The antagonists, however, see their disguises fall and are then condemned to suffer the wages of their sin — a sin which admits of no pardon, not because of its nature, but rather, due to the nature of its agent.

Given this fact and the complexity which we have seen in disguise, we may infer that the processes by which the society identifies its constituents and itself are in need of elucidation. We have raised significant and far-reaching questions as to the ways of identifying the essence, as opposed to the appearances, of character. Having seen the scope and dynamism of the disguise game in the text's society, we must wonder as to the dynamics of the system which attributes an inner, immutable identity to the members of that society and to the society as a whole. By way of addressing these and other issues pertaining to the processes of identification in *L'Astrée*, we shall turn our attention now to this system as it is set out in the text. We shall, ourselves, go beyond the illusions of disguise that entangle the perceptions of characters, in order to arrive at a fuller understanding of the manner in which "être" is labelled and codified for society and reader alike.

7. The Markers of Identity

The use of disguise in any literary work is obviously germane to the concept of identity. The identity of character indeed forms the foundation upon which disguise is contrived; it supplies the reality which the illusion tries to hide. In a text structured on a dynamic system of disguise, a clear understanding of the system of identity is crucial for the perception of its coherence. For this reason we embark on a study of the procedures of identification set out in *L'Astrée*.

Identity is one of the truths which illusion labors to falsify, the "être" enshrouded by the "paraître" which does not always give an accurate or reliable representation. The process of identification must therefore rest on an underlying principle which permits the text to establish the continuity of character, through a maze of illusions stretched over an enormously long and complicated narrative. This process endows the textual figure with the characteristics permitting recognition of a discrete, consistent unit of sense.

Identity and recognition go hand in hand. We speak of identity partly in terms of recognition: the identity of character is the sum total of the signs by which the character is recognized by others or by the reader; but the term also denotes the way in which the character defines and views himself or herself. In that sense, it is parallel to (or it includes) individuality, since the identity of character is that which sets that character apart from all others. It is not a static notion, but rather the result of a cumulative process which aggregates the signs acting as information.

We shall undertake the examination of identity in *L'Astrée*, in the various aspects which render it so complex a topic. Our investigation will be concerned with ways of establishing and maintaining true identity, as well as with processes of identification and recognition by characters and reader alike. We shall also consider how characters can be grouped with reference to these processes. For practical reasons, we shall restrict the scope of our survey to the primary and more important secondary characters in the work, setting aside the tertiary, almost insignificant figures, the crowds in the battle scenes or the groups of dancing girls — they contribute nothing to the understanding of identity and may be discounted by virtue of their lack of specific characteristic. Their function is to provide society with depth and breadth, but not to define it.

As an organic unit this society defines its own identity in two ways. We have already give some attention to the first which is the society's own hierarchical system of caste. The other element from which the society derives its definition is its pact with the gods, that is, its relationship with the supernatural. It will be the principal function of one group of characters (the druids) to elucidate this relationship, and consequently this role will be a decisive factor in the definition of their own identity.

This is a rather standard way of setting up social identity. In contrast, the identity of the individual in *L'Astrée* is a complex one. In the first place, we are not dealing with characters who would anticipate the later French tradition, that is, who would be depicted in great psychological, emotional, and even physical detail. Rather we encounter characters who are identified more by associative than by direct means. Instead of standing out as clearly delineated, individual entities, the characters of *L'Astrée* (and characters of the pastoral in history) are indeed, for the most part, types whose individuality often stems from a contingent function in the plot, rather than from a fundamental characteristic trait.

This is particularly clear with the text's many secondary characters. There are three basic processes by which they are supplied with an identity. The most frequently appealed to is identification by function alone, whereby they are recognized for the sole purpose of furthering the action through some deed. This deed alone provides the telling characteristic of identity. An astrologer offers counsel to Ursace and Olimbre (II, 557-558); after fulfilling his role, the astrologer disappears forever from the text without having ever shown any identifying trait other than his function as astrologer in that episode. This type of character is devoid of any personal or individual depth: aside from his function, he has no identity but that which may possibly be attributed to him by association with similar figures in the text. The astrologer could be grouped, and hence identified, with the other characters who deal in good faith with the supernatural, although no such association is made explicit.

Second among the ways in which the secondary characters are endowed with identity is that which marks unnamed figures with some distinct trait of personality. Such characters are thus clearly perceived to be different, even from those with similar functions. They become individuals with some differentiating depth of character, even if they have no name. Nonetheless their importance is restricted to the influence which they exert upon major characters, and they are not themselves central to a line of action. One such character is the little girl who helps Leonide to find shelter as she flees from Polemas (IV, 722 ff.). The girl takes on distinguishing traits (for example, sincerity and naiveté), but she never reappears in the text. The same is true for her mother who is set apart from other peasants, in that she is described as "sage et avisee pour une personne de sa condition" (IV, 724). Such a distinction is noteworthy because it enables the character to stand out, however slightly, from all other characters in her *condition*, the great frame of comparison.

The last major process of identification of secondary characters is naming. The characters who do bear a name are usually almost as important as the primary characters because they fill very active roles. The only difference is that they are not themselves the principal agents in the working out of a problem or project. However, the attribution of a name raises these characters to a high level of individuality, as the name adds a degree of verbal recognizability. The plot function is transcended through the proces of naming which anchors the character semiologically. It lends an identity sign that may be recalled later, and furthermore among secondary characters, this identity tends to be permanent and unquestionable since their names are not manipulated as are those of major characters.

Naturally there are gradations within each of these three types of processes affecting the lesser figures of *L'Astrée*. Among the unnamed characters who are identified solely by their functions, obviously some are more memorable (hence, recognizable and identifiable) than others: for example, the nameless guide who travels with Alcidon (III, 131 ff.) is of markedly less significance than the nameless messenger who sparks Alcidon's jealousy with remarks about his beloved (III, 153-154). Similarly, among the named secondary characters, certain nobles who are mentioned only in passing are of decidedly minor consequence in comparison with Halladin, the free-speaking squire of Damon.

It is a general rule in *L'Astrée* that unnamed characters do not reappear in the text after the episode in which they fulfill their specific function, and that their appearance is confined to a relatively small space in the text. Since it is primarily their functions which separate and distinguish them from other characters, function remains virtually their only identification. With characters at this level, there is little or no duality of function, showing great linearity of purpose and, as a result, singularity of identity.

Named secondary characters, on the other hand, often reappear after their initial introduction. With the advantage of a name to secure their identity, they are able to assume multiple functions. Halladin, for example, is alternately squire, counselor, messenger, and confidant of Damon. Function always accompanies name in *L'Astrée*, since no named character ever appears gratuitously. The reader can expect that if a character has a name, he or she will have a role that will affect the plot. Of course, function can undergo change, or even a reversal, as in the case of Semire who begins as an antagonist, but dies in the service of the heroes. A special case is that of servants: as may be expected of characters of lower social rank, they often derive a measure of their identity from their masters, and their masters' values are assumed as their own.

Naturally there are other traits of identity that are self-evident: gender, age, and social status; physical description also counts, but this descriptive element rarely appears in *L'Astrée*. All these, in the service of the secondary characters, are static traits. There is no play on them in the text's vast game of illusions and disguises. Given this lack of dynamism, little of interest remains to be said of identification for secondary characters; however, the topic becomes more interesting in the cases of the text's major characters.

The same processes are used for the identification of both echelons, but those processes become greatly more complex when serving to identify the more central characters. As one may well suppose, the major characters are endowed with more depth and variety of activity and expression, which gives them a more specific identity. An added factor here, the notion of recognition among characters, was not pertinent to our treatment of secondary characters.

As we consider the processes of identification for characters of substance, we will divide them into two groups: the first will be the objective markers, ostensibly fixed and taken to be an inherent part of the character; the other will be the external subjective markers, more changeable and not taken to be inborn. The detailed study of these two groups of markers will, it is hoped, elucidate the processes by which characters are recognized both in society and by the reader.

Obviously we have chosen not to include narratorial attributes as indicators of identity. This choice has been made for two main reasons. First, qualities attributed by the narrator are a sign for the reader only, affixed to the character but not borne in society; second, the master narrator is both selective and sometimes misleading in his commentary, and all narrators (especially the secondary ones) can be biased with regard to a given character. Consequently, we have decided to take out as much as possible the various narrators' editorializing from the identification process, and to consider identity as a set of markers that derive their meaning from society as depicted in the text.

Objective Markers of Identity

1. Name is the most evident marker of recognition which a character bears, and it is naturally the one upon which the narrator relies most often in order to summon that recognition from the reader. Once a character receives a name in the narrative, this name can act as a pointer to his or her true identity beneath any disguise and in any circumstance: the first name given to a character by the narrator is the true one for narrative purposes. The narrator is careful to observe this principle with regard to the reader, even when other characters labor under false assumptions. The only two exceptions concern the Silvandre/Paris identity exchange, and the true identity of Rosileon which remains a secret (until IV, 639). The names "Silvandre" and "Rosileon" are aliases borne in the absence of true names, and the characters as well as the reader are aware of this fact all along.

Despite the concreteness of the name and the narrative pact of accuracy that develops with respect to the initial naming of characters, this marker is not always reliable. The name, indeed, is not kept safe from the kinds of game playing which beset many of the other identity markers. The narrator can play with names or endow characters with new ones: the name of Alexis overtly supplants the true name of Celadon; a pseudonym can temporarily hide an already familiar character, as occurs with the "Chevalier du Tygre" who is finally recognized as Damon (III, 636); it also happens occasionally that the narrator withholds the name of a character for a while. Thus, while the reader is virtually always apprised of the true name of a character, this identification can prove to be a source of difficulty among the characters themselves. Names can be borrowed or invented in support of other illusions, failing to guarantee an identification; the entire procedure of identification seeks to be more penetrating in this textual world of disguise and illusion.

In spite of any unreliability, the name remains the central identifying sign. Besides, as a sign, it is not at all neutral: some names bear obvious cratyllic value, and others, mythological references. Among lovers, names are often carved into trees or reduced to insignias, thus lending a kind of permanence or codified substance to the denotative power of the name.

As for the names bearing cratyllic value, the unreliability of the sign is underscored by the connotative capacity of the name in certain cases. Most obvious is the example of Astrée whose name is that of the spirit of Justice in mythology.[1] In light of her harsh treatment of Celadon, not to mention her begrudging and jealous nature, no character is less deserving to be identified with the spirit of Justice. Adamas as well is not as flawless as the diamond which his name signifies in Latin, and Silvandre (we are told explicitly) is "silvan" only in his costume, as his manners bespeak noble birth and cultured upbringing.

2. The society is carefully codified according to gender, and not only in a grammatical sense, although this is certainly the most basic form of linguistic identification; we are speaking specifically of identity as a function of sexuality. The definition of character is, in many circumstances, determined by the exigencies and constraints imposed on his or her sex by social conventions. In all but a few exceptional cases, the male and female attributes (regarding expected conduct, tastes, etc.) are constant and predetermined: men are physically strong, greatly sensitive to codes of honor and love, courageous and courteous, poor at hiding their feelings, and above all, susceptible to falling hopelessly in love; women are beautiful, subtly flirtatious while affecting a mein of severity, sensitive to the charge of honor in sexuality, decisive and discerning, and, as women, they are portrayed somewhat unflatteringly as secretive and prone to covert action. As groups, then, the men show impulsiveness, faithfulness and obedience, whereas

---

[1] See Gilbert Highet, *The Classical Tradition* (New York and London: Oxford University Press, 1949) 170.

the women are reflective, insightful, and discreet. The exceptions to these generalities are rare characters provided with a dynamic force which, for the most part, turns them into antagonists. As a rule, conduct, attributes, and predilections are determined along sexual lines.

So rigid is this delineation that it supplies the text with its most interesting and powerful form of illusion. As has been shown in our study of transsexual disguise, the outward appearances of either sex bring along with them many of that gender's inner qualities as well: men "become" women and vice versa, not only in appearance but in attribute too. This is why identification along sexual lines, in spite of its ostensible objectivity, is not a stable process of classification: the lines can be crossed too easily.

One of the text's most explicit definitions of male identity is stated by Damon's squire, Halladin. While describing woman as being "d'un naturel soubmis et flechissant" (traits which do not, incidentally, befit the women of this pastoral society), he does go on to add that manhood commands one necessarily to be courageous (III, 31). There are few other passages in *L'Astrée* which verbalize these (or other) aspects of masculinity with such clarity; the code is unwritten, but known nonetheless. One is not left to wonder about the issue since the code of manhood is often alluded to implicitly, as would be a matter of common knowledge. Each male is aware of what is expected of his conduct, and this is an important aspect of his qualification for membership in society.

The principal definition of masculine identity according to improper or antagonistic standards (hence inimical to heroic standards) is offered by the eunuch Heracle to his master, emperor Valentinian (II, 519). In short, Heracle portrays the masculinity of the royal personnage as a function of lust and brute force. Halladin's and Heracle's opposite standards are offset by the lighthearted *libertinage* of Hylas, the lone exponent of sex without commitment, whom no one takes seriously. In light of the negative images offered by Heracle and Hylas, the implicit positive code underlying the issue everywhere else, and the ancient traditions of pastoral literature, the definition of proper masculine conduct is never in doubt.

The standards of femininity, on the other hand, are at once more vague and even more normative than those propounded for male characters. Women are expected to be concerned with the preservation of honor for the sake of appearances, although clandestine love affairs are quite commonplace. As women, they are identified by their beauty and romantic involvement: for example, other characters tend to describe them in narration first by their beauty and likeliness to attract men, before speaking of their family identities or their values. In short, they are known by their actual potential attractiveness to the opposite sex, thus femininity derives its identity indirectly from masculinity, although the converse situation does not obtain. Nowhere is this more clearly seen than in the case of Celidée who disfigures herself in order to be less attractive: as a woman, she is identified by her beauty and she tries to alter this identity. Elsewhere, Stelle is summarily typified as being less beautiful than the average shepherdess; the women of Forez are categorized as being more beautiful than others, and so on.

Ultimately gender is a characteristic which underlies all appearances but which, in spite of its inherent immutability, does not provide a reliable external marker of identification. Each sex has traits and behavioral characteristics (or standards) that are assumed to accompany that sex; but the potential for illusion is provided by the fact that these attributes are neither inborn nor inimitable. Furthermore, the subtle motif of androgyny, which is an evident trait (along with innocence, youth and beauty) of both sexes in the narrative, makes something of a problem for differentiation by gender, as we have had occasion to note above.

In an obvious effort to clarify or give uniformity to gender identity, the society attempts to sequester each of the sexes away from the other. Temple rites are reserved for women; friendship is valued between members of the same sex; etc. As a matter of social convention, the society is arranged into homogeneous groups, but there is constant pressure from within to break these categories and to establish a heterogeneous order. Hence the awkwardness and game playing that mark virtually all heterosexual relationships but are noticeably absent from relationships between members of the same sex.

Finally, there is an underlying motif of latent homosexuality in the text, a motif which corresponds to and derives from the systematic group segregation accepted by each sex. No doubt one could explain away the numerous instances of female characters exchanging "caresses," or of members of the same sex who prefer each other's company to that of the other sex.[2] But the ambiguity of the text's position on

---

[2] An unlikely example is Hylas whose remarks (II, 172) in this regard seem strange coming from such a renowned womanizer. See also III, 238 and 247.

this issue remains: on the one hand, both Adamas (III, 499) and shortly thereafter Silvandre (III, 509) try to minimize any homosexual overtones in the society's activities; on the other hand, Alexis, already in transsexual disguise, responds to a thinly veiled intimation of homosexuality by saying that Nature "veut que chacun aime son semblable" (III, 275). Note that both Silvandre and Alexis appeal to Nature as the basis of their arguments.

The issue is at the center of what is perhaps the most extraordinary passage of *L'Astrée*. It is the moment when Alexis embraces Astrée with "caresses...plus serées que celles que les filles ont accoustumé de se faire" (III, 598) inspiring jealousy on the part of Leonide and Diane, and eliciting a rather spirited response in Astrée. Astrée, while seeing in Alexis the "living portrait" of Celadon, hides in shame when a knock is heard at the door. Does Astrée feel guilty for responding to the advances of a man or of a woman in this passage? The answer is unclear here, just as the entire issue of sexuality is unclear throughout the text.

It is evident that the component of sexuality in the identity of character is in a state of confusion. The society seems involved in an effort to redefine sexual affinities as it moves from a homogeneous grouping pattern to a heterogeneous one. At the center of the issue is each character's concept of self, but it projects on the surrounding society. The best illustration of this crisis will be visible later in our detailed discussion of Celadon.

3. Like the preceding marker of identity, ancestry also offers a concept which appears to be stable and yet is susceptible to play. According to the accepted social code, one is as one is born, and this is taken to be as valid an identifying trait as any. Ancestry is looked upon by society as a fixed and immutable identity marker: one assumes the social identity of one's parents and, ideally, accepts it as permanent and binding. But there are two sources of confusion in this process.

The first involves the notion of unknown parentage, common in pastoral literature: two major characters here, Silvandre and Rosileon, are affected. In Silvandre's case, the "lock" of ancestry has a detrimental effect on his romantic aspirations since his beloved Diane's family will not permit her to marry a "personne incognue" (III, 245) — the "incognue" part refers not to the man, but to his ancestry. The family's reaction reveals Silvandre's overall standing in the society of Forez, inasmuch as he is always regarded as an outsider. He is first seen near the beginning of the romance, as an intruder in search of the ancestral roots of which he is deprived, and he is consequently looked upon by all as an unknown — an indication of the fact that one is socially identified by one's ancestral heritage.

The same is largely true in the case of Rosileon who, without the recognition of his royal lineage, is forced to work his way out of slavery toward his manifest destiny as a king. Throughout the narrative, both he and Silvandre respond to the noble "cri du sang" which reveals their inner and unknown identities; but in society they are without a past, without foundation, and thus bereft of any permanent identity.

The second problem undermining ancestry as a means of identification involves the question of mobility. As has been seen in the examination of social disguise, the barriers erected around social classes may be overcome through the use of illusion. In a sense, the shepherd society of the Lignon is actually engaging in such an illusion as it exchanges an initially noble status and courtly life for the tranquility of the rustic existence: we are explicitly told that the shepherds who populate Forez do descend from noble blood (II, 311). Other means are available to the prospective social climber: Celadon, for example, is repeatedly urged by Galathée to consent to marriage above his caste, with the idea that such a promotion would be generally accepted. Of course, were he to yield to her entreaties, he would belie his ancestry and consequently change his identity, or, as he phrases it, "se rendre autre chose que ce qu'il estoit" (I, 381).

There is therefore a hierarchy of blood according to which the society classifies its members, but this order is neither infallible nor unchanging. Besides, whereas the nobility of blood could be expected to carry along with it a noble purity of intent, the contrary is early shown to be the case: Polemas, for example, is introduced by Leonide in terms of "race" which "en noblesse ne cede pas mesme à Galathée" (I, 324), and yet he proves to be the arch-villain of the text; similarly, virtually all of the kings portrayed in *L'Astrée* are thoroughly corrupt. In short, good and evil coexist within the ranks of each "race" and thus ancestry cannot supply a reliable moral identification of character. This breakdown in the identification process is often a source of consternation for characters who naturally seek correlatives between the ancestral and the moral scales.

4. Implicitly associated with the ancestry marker is that of social status which is understood by the society to be a function of ancestry. With very few exceptions the social status of a character is inherited

from his or her parents. Ostensibly the lines of separation between social classes are as fixed as a character's parentage. However, this marker shares a degree of unreliability with ancestry because both can be subverted by the same means of illusion. Status is understood to be the present-time indicator of parentage: the present generation is at least supposed to be as the previous one was. When such is not the case, appearances belie the inner reality for some specific reason, be it in the service of good or of evil. This marker is used by society for the purpose of classifying individuals, but the process is, as we have seen, subject to the force of disguise.

Considered in this light, status contributes to the perceived identity of character in that it often predetermines the kinds of activity in which the individual is engaged. The overwhelming majority of characters are also quick to identify themselves in their own eyes by social rank, seeing in it a code which articulates what is expected of them. A noble identifies with the courtly code as much as with other nobles. In similar fashion, the shepherd sees himself necessarily bound to the "vie champestre," and defines himself according to rustic values and mores. And social rank serves to define lower-class characters (servants, maids, squires, etc.) as reflections of their superiors. There are, of course, concrete cases which undermine this scheme, such as that of Leriane, the perfidious servant.

5. It is hard to conceive that physical attribute, which would come to constitute a major identity marker in later centuries, could be of as little import as it is in *L'Astrée*. Yet there is scarcely a single character of major stature who is identified to the reader primarily in physical terms. We have no idea of the physiognomy of Celadon or Astrée (except that the latter is beautiful), nor are we told of their bodily appearance (save that Celadon becomes thin after his banishment). This lack of physical detail is a general rule carefully followed in the narrative: we know, for example, that Lydias and Ligdamon resemble each other facially and corporally to an astonishing degree, and yet both remain faceless to the reader.

Under the heading of physical description we include all the customary generic recognition marks: scars, birthmarks, etc. For example, it is finally a scar that provides the only means of differentiating between Lydias and Ligdamon (IV, 767). Clothing is also included here, but it is not a particularly telling marker either. Clothing is consistently much more an indicator of social class than of individual identity; characters wear the garb of their caste, but singular identity needs to be made more precise. On occasion, clothing provides the means for an identity exchange, but does not clarify the identification process for the individual. We are told, for example, that Celadon and his brother Lycidas often exchange clothes (II, 275), but we are not informed of anything distinctive about the dress of either character. In short, clothing contributes to the process of social identification but not to that of the individual.

In keeping with the ostensible platonic code of the text the physical aspect of character is greatly downplayed in favor of the ideal and the moral. In much the same way that love is most often idealized (instead of stressing the erotic component), identity too is not primarily a physically based phenomenon in the narrative: in large measure the members of the pastoral society prefer not to dwell on their physical existence, but rather to transcend it in order to live in the abstract domain of storytelling, reverie, idealized love, or even madness. The ordinary interpersonal relationship — be it love or the process of identification — is not essentially fulfilled or validated on the physical plane: witness the ease with which physical disguise is effected, or the repeated inability of old acquaintances to recognize each other visually (for example, Hylas and Hermante in III, 57).

As regards the physical aspect of character, we are almost always left with the most general descriptions pointing to sexual or social classification rather than to individual identity. Physical attributes for men serve only to underscore their ability to fight (or, on occasions of disguise, to blend in with women). Some men are categorized as stronger than others; some excel at olympic games; but again, these traits do not set up a consistent gradient for markers of identity.

In striking contrast with this general lack of physical detail is the unique character of Hylas. In his case alone we are repeatedly told that he has red hair (that is, what is left of his hair, since he is bald), and that this characteristic sets him apart from all other men in the society. Red hair in the traditional literary semiology does indeed connote singularity or strangeness, reflecting a passionate nature or even insanity. But with Hylas the singularity of red hair stands out even more because of the fact that the text is elsewhere so stringent with any degree of detail in physical description: Celiodante is the only other character in *L'Astrée* whose hair color is mentioned for the narrative record (IV, 638).

The sparsity of physical detail affects the female characters as well as the male. We are told that certain are more beautiful than others and that, as a general rule, women of high social rank are taken to be more attractive than their social inferiors. The notable exception to this tenet is the shepherd society of the Lignon, whose women (to the surprise of many foreign visitors) are found to be more comely than even the circle of Nymphs. This is of course another way of underscoring the inherent nobility of the Lignon society, since here as elsewhere the women and men of the shepherd caste rival their courtly counterparts. But the noteworthy point is that physical detail, as far as the narrative expresses it, is relative to the world within the text: we may know that a woman is beautiful, but we have no idea what the traits of beauty are.

We have previously mentioned that characters' disguises across sexual lines often adopt physical attributes of the opposite sex: women become proficient fighters, men assume feminine voices, and so on. The identifying factor of physical attribute must thus be sufficiently flexible to lend support to this type of disguise. The same is true in the case of social disguise, when nymphs are not recognized in the dress of peasants. Since identity traits are either altered or threatened by disguise, it is evident that identification through physical means forms neither a reliable nor a practical process in the pastoral society.

6. A character's past, when it is formally introduced in the narrative either by the master narrator or through intercalated narration, may be seen as a means of specifying identity. It is important because the pastoral society places much value on the notion of heritage — both ancestral and social. It is true that the majority of characters who have a part in the current action of *L'Astrée* are endowed with a past told at some point, and thus are provided with some foundation for a chronological as well as motivational depth. Of course, since the past of almost every character is related in the text, the process itself can hardly be seen as a significant way of setting certain characters apart from the rest. Certain prominent figures like Sigismond, the good son of the villainous king Gondebaut, have no narrated past. Hence it is no mark of great textual distinction for a character to have his or her past made known.

7. The characters of *L'Astrée* are inveterate readers of each other's writings, and the text records a great number of letters and "stances" which are reported to exist in written form. For this reason, handwriting is viewed by the characters as a means of identification; at many points we are told of one recognizing the writing of another, and of course, that writing is frequently considered to be tantamount

to the presence of the writer. Celadon's concern for the letters of Astrée illustrate this point (see I, 66). Writing provides a presence in actual absence, a phenomenon to which the idealizing society of *L'Astrée* is very sensitive. Writing thus becomes an act of signature or statement of identity which appears to exist separately and apart from the author.

Given the privileged position accorded in this society to writing, one might thus be tempted to categorize it as a tangible identity marker upon which characters may truly rely. However, a complication arises in the use of handwriting as a sign of recognition: it is a sign which can be forged or misread. Silvandre, for example, manages at one point to mistake Celadon's writing for his own (II, 86). In another episode, which turns completely on the identification of handwriting, Celadon falls for a forgery of Astrée's writing, runs away and is found only after his brother Lycidas recognizes his handwriting on a letter floating in a river (I, 143-145). Such a juxtaposition of unsuccessful and successful uses of writing as an identity marker only points to the inconsistency which makes it unreliable in the end.

The uncertainty besetting this marker casts it in with all of the others that we have examined up to this point. All of them can be played upon in some way, leaving the society (but not the reader) as yet without a sound and objective way of permanently identifying its constituents. In fact, only three such markers have come to our attention, and we shall turn to them now.

8. The age of a character, if it is given or implied, is never put into doubt. We are led to believe (and we have no reason not to believe) that virtually all characters are in the prime of their youth; if a given character is not, then we are told so without equivocation. No suspicion is ever cast on this marker, and no illusion in the text uses the guise of age change as its vehicle.

In clearly positive characters, advanced age is generally made out to be sign of commensurate wisdom and benevolence. This is certainly the case with regard to Adamas or Avite (the avuncular governor of Sigismond, IV, 448 ff.), but the trait is not reserved to a particular social level. There are good peasants for whom old age functions in the same way, as in the case of the old man who offers advice and aid to Dorinde (IV, 432) or the old woman who harbors Leonide (IV, 724 ff.). These characters are positive types; in the text's more neutral characters, old age or youth is not significant or symbolic.

There is one story in *L'Astrée* where old age plays a crucial role: the story of Thamire which furnishes an interesting variation on the familiar theme of true love. Thamire, much older than his beloved Celidée, competes for her love against a young man, and yet he is chosen by her out of love (II, 28 ff.). This is the only occasion in the entire text where love is mutual across a gap in age. In other situations of misalliance in age, seniority is viewed as a negative factor and the elderly man is seen as a negative force.

9. Geographic origins are often brought up in the narrative either by narrator or character as a means of identifying or defining a character. The character's geographic origins provide another element of identity to refer to his or her past, and constitute thus a process similar to identification by ancestry or social status. But unlike these two, no illusion plays on characters' place of birth, and this information is often used as a reliable classification.

One interesting fact in this regard is that almost all of the knights and ladies who appear in Forez come from outside the area, and do so either in flight or in urgent quest. In contrast, those who are originally of the area have been insulated from the concerns of politics, and they remain so until the great crisis in the text's fourth volume. Forez thus enjoys the aspect of a utopia which, isolated from the political affairs surrounding it, can be the focus of such contemplative pursuits as storytelling and the idealization of love.

In spite of the fact that most characters who assemble on the "stage" of Forez are out of their own native area, virtually all of them maintain their identity of geographic origin. These figures are either rustic or courtly, and reference is often made in individual cases to their status in this respect. Several "foreigners" voice a desire to assimilate into the Forez lifestyle, but Paris is the only one who commits himself in that direction — and his effort is too overt and self-conscious to be serious. Therefore the trait of one's place of birth remains a factor in the composite identity of character.

10. We can identify characters by their roles as poets or storytellers — whether they have such a role, and what type of story they relate. Virtually all stories, however, deal with past events and are told for the sake of bringing other characters (and the reader) up to date in the action, and thus there is little variance in the function of storytelling. The significant distinguishing or identifying traits are to be

found in the actual narration process: certain narrators color or characterize their stories in certain ways. Hylas, for example, tends to tell stories in a humorous way in keeping with his personality. Dorinde, on the other hand, tends to season her narrative with a good measure of antimasculine sentiment. The only story which Adamas relates is the chronicle of illustrious dynasties. Other characters, such as Fossinde (IV, 116 ff.), exist solely for the purpose of telling the stories of others, and are attributed the role of narrators by virtue of the fact that they are "reliable" and uninvolved in the events that they are to recount. The manner and content of narration function as a sign of differentiation among characters, and may thus be viewed as a marker of identity.

Subjective Markers of Identity

The other type of identity marker in *L'Astrée* is extrinsic, that is to say, not part of the character's intrinsic makeup. Unlike those which we have just examined, these traits are changeable in themselves and are not necessarily taken by the reader or by other characters to be of an objective quality. Neither are they of an inborn nature, as were most of those considered above. The processes of identification to which we now turn are those chosen by the individual, and thus may be abandoned or may change. It is these which are ultimately of more importance within the society as individuals seek a dependable way of qualifying each other. This is due principally to two factors: first, as indicated above, the objective identity markers as a group are prone to breakdown; second, the subjective markers about to be considered are more perceptible and tangible, since they deal with character behavior in a society that is somewhat oblivious to outward signs — this, we repeat, is a matter of generic tradition.

1. Whether a character stands on the side of good, that is, whether the character participates in the general efforts of the text's heroes, is a primary means of identification in the pastoral tradition and in *L'Astrée* in particular. In this romance, individuals are classified by their stance on questions of the general good, propriety and social order, and classified by these parameters within a society that is most attentive to its moral priorities. For the reader, this is one of the steadiest types of identification of characters who are strongly involved one way or the other in this issue. For the characters themselves, this position provides a key technique of peer identification, giving them their principal denominator for identifying with one another and for the

formation of groups. Those who are on the side of good do their best to expose evil in their midst and to draw the lines of identification clearly.

Most characters are among the good; only a handful qualify as major antagonists: Polemas and his henchmen, Climante, Ardilan, Leriane, Gondebaut, and most of the other kings who appear in the action. The principal reason for reliance upon the moral marker is that it is rarely played upon: the lines between extreme good and evil are drawn so heavily that there is little middle ground on which to build an illusion. With exceptional accuracy, each character knows where others stand on the issue; and the issue induces each one to show his or her true colors with remarkable consistency. In those very few cases where these moral credentials are falsified, the illusion involves one of the disguises already enumerated in our study.

The moral distinction must be understood here only in its most general terms; only characters who are clearly for or against the central heroes and heroines will be clearly positive or negative characters. But not all fine aspects of the moral system are precisely defined and uniformly adhered to. In the first place, there are flaws in some positive characters whose guilt is attenuated by a sort of common consent: it was pointed out, for example, that Lycidas is lightly forgiven for his affair with Olimpe and for her resulting pregnancy; it can also be argued that Adamas, the main moral spokesman, is not entirely consistent with other voices for the heroic code.[3] Furthermore, a character may change — something of a rarity in the pastoral tradition, — not in an evolving fashion, but rather in a sudden switch to the good, as occurs in the case of Semire.

2. Since one of the great character types of the pastoral is the lover, one must include as an identity marker in *L'Astrée* the character's status as a lover. This trait subdivides: first, if the love is proper or improper, and second, if the love is requited or not.

Despite the fact that the code of proper love is not completely fixed, and even though it admits of much discussion, there is nonetheless a universally understood notion of what constitutes the correct conduct and intentions of love. Most, but not all, characters accept it. Those who do not have varied motivations: some reject the code out of malice or evil intent; others do so out of lust; and still others seek to use love as a means to another end. For whatever reason, such

---

[3] See Gregorio, "Implications of the Love Debate."

characters are branded both to the reader and to fellow characters as renegades whose entire identity is altered for that fact. Calidon (who loves Celidée only for her beauty) and Tirinte (who uses trickery and force with Silvanire, IV, 128 ff.) illustrate the point; both of these characters are castigated for their misunderstanding of love and its proper way.

Most of the young lovers are loved in return and thus are able to identify (that is, to be identified) with the object of love, through this mutual affection. The text actually proposes a theory of the ideal lover who seeks to "become" the beloved, and thus identify with her (II, 262-264). Celadon does find his own identifying traits in Astrée because she takes over much of his consciousness and forms much of his *raison d'être*. However, even proper love is sometimes not mutual, and another subtype of character is formed: the character (male or female, as there are examples of both) whose love is not requited. Such figures stand apart in *L'Astrée*, identifying only in absence with the beloved. Because they are such rare cases, their unrequited love becomes a telling trait of identity in its own right.

3. Parallel to the poles of positive and negative love, embodied in the lover and the nonlover, another polarized typology of character functions as an equally effective identity marker. It refers to a behavioral spectrum, one extreme of which is the trickster or joker, and the other extreme an introverted, melancholic hero. All characters are not defined according to these extremes, but all find a place along an axis between the two poles.

Hylas and Stelle are good examples of the extreme of the trickster type, although Hylas acts out of a sense of humor whereas Stelle is sometimes motivated by malice. On the other side, an illustration of total seriousness (almost to the point of humorlessness) is personified by Silvandre, and complete melancholy is typified by Tircis who never overcomes the death of his beloved (I, 248 ff.). The great majority of characters are situated between such extremes. The ordinarily sober Astrée, for example, is able to play pranks with her friends — pranks which, incidentally, turn on the notion of identity (as in IV, 72-75). Diane instigates a similar identity joke targeted at Adamas (III, 596). Even Celadon/Alexis is able to humor Hylas' perennial declarations of love, simply for the sake of having fun (II, 464 ff.). Thus a character's degree of willingness to play tricks furnishes a trait which separates him or her from others along a graduated scale.

4. A character may be identified, and hence grouped, by his or her general goals which supply an outward and variable marker. There are scarcely any characters in *L'Astrée* whose presence is gratuitous since each one has a goal or purpose which motivates actions. Sometimes it is even the sole determiner of actions, especially when the characters pursue their goals with singularity of intent. But even when the goal is not totally compelling, there remains that the overwhelming majority of actors are involved in some kind of project which directs them to a general end, thus serving as an identity marker.

Many characters are on a pilgrimage in the text, and they appear in Forez just long enough to tell the story of their quest, whatever it may be. The general goals of these pilgrimages may be grouped into types which have some relevance even to those figures who do not travel in a search of some sort.

Some seek judgment or arbitration; others seek love in one form or another; still others are in search of combat, while some come to be cured of illness. These and other general goals are found in all characters of stature, though they may coexist in various combinations and degrees of intensity. In each case, they may be seen to differentiate one character from another and to provide a measure of individuality with respect to types of purpose. For this reason, a general goal serves for characters and reader alike as a means of focusing fragments of information around one individual, thus calling attention to his or her uniqueness.

5. Closely related to the notion of goals is that of narrative function, involving the reader. Characters may be categorized by the complexity of their function, that is to say, by the degree of their involvement in one or a multiplicity of activities on which the narrative rests. It is indeed an identification process, given the fact that no single character (as opposed to a group, such as dancing girls, armies, etc.) appears in the narrative without at least one specific narrative function. In this regard, *L'Astrée* (like all pastorals before it) shows great consistency and economy.

The actual types of activity may be divided along various standards. For the sake of simplicity and concision, it will suffice to consider only the most general ones, yielding three types of characters.

First is the active type. This is usually the fighter, the assertive one who is a doer rather than a thinker. To use Celadon as an example, we see that, in the pursuit of his goals, he is inclined toward action.

Instead of forging his own standards or challenging the "idées reçues" of society, he accepts those of society. He takes a part in society's games of illusion, engages in combat when called upon, and actively pursues his beloved — all the while echoing the common set of values without articulating any original thought on the subject.

Conversely, the second type is the passive character who, rather than effectively reacting to situations, indulges in introspective considerations. This is the contemplative figure, the thinker who, unlike his active counterpart, has ideas of his own and phrases them in original terms. Silvandre is the exemplary passive character: he deals in words, in ideas and in abstractions, settling his differences by argumentation rather than by violence. This type of character actually sets the standards and values for society instead of merely following them. Many of the text's female characters belong to this category.

The third type of activity worthy of attention is situated between the two extremes of active and passive roles. This is the intermediary function of the arbiter, best exemplified by Adamas. His function in the society is two-fold: he administers justice between adversaries, but also mediates between the society as a whole and its gods. The chief druid is not alone in this category. Several other characters are called upon temporarily to play the role of arbiter. This circumstance underscores a phenomenon observed in several other identity markers: characters may be identified by the combination of elements which they embody in respect to a given marker. This is an indication that the characters of *L'Astrée* are not as typecast as one may first suspect.

6. An identifying distinction may be drawn from the examination of the company which a character keeps. Information about a previously unknown figure in the text may be extrapolated from the knowledge of which other characters he or she associates with. Like the other external and variable markers considered up to this point, this one is associated with character typology: most frequently a character will choose his circle of associates according to his own social or moral type. However, this marker is practically reserved for the reader who is enabled to group characters by virtue of the chosen circle of contact. Without having previously encountered Ligonias, Peledonte, Argonide, or Lystandre, the reader is able to categorize them as villains because they consort with Polemas; this particular association is made along lines of moral type.

7. The last of the variable identification markers is the only one which can be truly said not to be related to (or a function of) the typology of character. It consists of the character's family relationships and marital status. The question is whether he or she has close family ties (if indeed there are any at all), whether he or she is married, betrothed, etc., whether he or she is a parent. One might even include information concerning a character's sexual experience, although this aspect of identity might fall under other rubrics. All of these qualifications offer individualizing information about a personage — and all are significant in a text in which characteristic differentiation is sparse, and in which the overall society seems far more important than the individual.

These are the headings under which the reader, like the pastoral society, gathers differentiating information about individual characters. The information is comprised of details that combine to form the composite sketch, the fingerprint that states the individuality of characters in a society of types. In the coming chapter, we propose to examine the composite identities that set certain important characters apart. We propose to illustrate the identification process in a text born of a literary tradition which does not yet make use of a Balzacian sort of exhaustive, narrative portraiture. Such a narrative is *L'Astrée* in which association and affinity count for more than direct attribute.

8. Characters and Their Markers

Shepherds and nobles alike fall back on an inventory of identification markers, relying on any combination of these markers to categorize, qualify and identify each other, all with varying degrees of success. Taking notice of both fixed and variable markers, one character will arrive at a tacit typological understanding of another character — an important process for social dealings in a context where illusion is the order of the day.

The complex identification system falls short of its intended end, since characters fall for false appearances or because they fail to read properly the markers that they encounter. In spite of the abundance of identity markers, characters are never totally sure of each other. Aside from the ready devices of disguise and illusion, identity markers may be unreliable for many reasons: characters may live long under wrong identities, absence tends to obscure recognition, mistakes are made in perception, resemblances play havoc, and so on. Ultimately, the obvious does not always prevail, and appearances are shown time and again not to portray reality.

Under ideal circumstances, a study of *L'Astrée*'s identification processes would involve at this stage a careful assembly of the identity of all important characters. But such an undertaking would lead us to lengths rivaled only by the text of *L'Astrée* itself. Instead, let us propose to limit our study to a few central figures which illustrate the complexity and ultimate unreliability of the identification process in some exemplary way. We shall see principally that the marker by which a character is recognized is often not genuine, even when the character is acting in good faith. The reader, like some exceptionally well-informed characters, is able to recognize disguise upon encountering it, seeing it as an outer mask serving some social purpose. The mask may even be symbolic of a whole way of life for the pastoral society, but it is not to be taken at its face value. And then, there exist inner masks — masks that hide characters' true natures from themselves. These the reader has difficulty with, as they are indeed a part of a subtle game played by characters when they assume "roles," in the Sartrian meaning of the word. So let us proceed to the composite identities of five of *L'Astrée*'s most important figures, in an effort to spell out the roles they assume, what is expected of them, and how they are recognizable to society.

Galathée, the Social and Political Symbol

For our reading of the text, Galathée is one of the most interesting characters to appear. Confusion seems to reign in her identification processes. No doubt, her ostensible markers pose no great problem: one learns very early on that she is "la principale" of the nymphs of Isoure, that she is a princess and the daughter of queen Amasis. Consequently, she has a clear position defined by the coordinates referred to as the objective or intrinsic markers of identity. Her name and gender signs remain constant, and her ancestry and social status are always acknowledged by all. Her age and physical description are, as with all the text's characters, imprecise, but obviously she is young and beautiful. Her geographic origins are known to the reader. Her personal past is related by the intercalated narrative of Leonide (I, 323 ff.). Finally, she is neither poet nor storyteller, and her handwriting does not serve as a means of identification.

In spite of all that, Galathée shows a crisis of identification involving variable, external markers and their relationship to her true nature. She plays a special role in society because of her completely symbolic function. To the other characters, as well as to the reader, she represents outwardly the ideal member of the ruling caste. Identifying with the image of the perfect princess, she demands respect and deference from her social inferiors, and does nothing to discourage others from seeing and treating her as their superior. In this symbolic function she sets standards of conduct for others. She often speaks knowledgeably about priorities in ethics and etiquette. In questions pertaining to social order, where her own judgment is insufficient, there are several other standards which are expressly offered to her, most notably the pronouncements of Adamas and the advice of other nobles. But the entire society, nobles and shepherds, look to her as the noble "type" *par excellence*, and, given her situation, she is naturally more than aware of the "code de noblesse" and of what is expected of her as a princess and future queen. She represents this code to society, for she exemplifies its set of values, and it is clear that she identifies with it outwardly.

Yet she betrays that code of nobility both in thought and in deed, and, by the same token, she undermines the identity which she enjoys in the eyes of society. The reader can hardly miss the disparity between the two faces of this problematic character. The first occasion for doubts is brought about by her attempt to justify a misalliance between herself and Celadon. It is a well-known aspect of Celadon's identity that his family is of noble extraction, and on these grounds Galathée could conceivably have had a case, albeit not strong enough to convince Adamas and her peers. But Galathée does not argue on these grounds; instead she appeals to an unclear notion of a hierarchy of natural (not ancestral) merit worthy of Dioclétien in Rotrou's *Saint Genest*. Galathée says to Celadon: "...en quelque lieu que la vertu se trouve, elle merite d'estre aimée et honorée, aussi bien sous les habits des bergers, que sous la glorieuse pourpre des rois" (I, 47). Later she presses Celadon with claims of "Nature" (in an argument reminiscent of the one offered by l'Infante in Corneille's *Le Cid*) when, of course, "Nature" opposes any union between her and the shepherd: "Mais la loy de la nature precede toute autre: ceste loy nous commande de rechercher nostre bien, et pouvez vous en desirer un plus grand que celuy de mon amitié?" (I, 438).

At odds with the social order she increasingly symbolizes, Galathée attempts to influence Celadon by exhorting him to aspire to social advancement (I, 102). It is all the more incongruous because her personal and individual well-being is clearly associated with that of the society of Forez. She is the focus of the society's collective identity; and the society identifies with her even more than with her mother, the queen, because Galathée mixes with the people, and hence is much more visible and accessible to them. Given this unique symbolic function of personifying society's self-image, any attempt on Galathée's part to undermine the social order must be viewed as a denial of this function — in other words, an inner mask with which Galathée hides a part of her true identity from herself, denying her highly symbolic status.

The disparity goes further. While she stands outwardly in favor of the good as it is defined by the bearers of positive values, she also tries to mute the various voices which point out the proper way to her — most notably that of Leonide (I, 71). Moreover, she abuses her authority by constraining Celadon to remain in her presence. The confusion mounts into a tension between what Galathée purports to be and is taken to be, on the one hand, and that which she shows herself to be, on the other.

In light of her symbolic status, any shortcoming which she exhibits will cause confusion in the process of identification, as far as moral and political values are concerned. As it turns out, she is duped a second time by the false druid Climante (II, 292), despite the fact that she is aware of his fakery. But later in the text, she is able to laugh at the fear which Climante inspires in the other nymphs (IV, 658), testifying to some duplicity in her attitude toward the false mystic as she wavers between credulity and criticism. Standing, as she does, on the side of the heroes and the good, she raises questions about her true nature when she hedges in the least regarding the central issue of religious practices.

In short, a curious double-nature marks the character of Galathée, generating a tension between her ostensible appearance (even to herself) and her behavior in certain situations. Perhaps the clearest illustration of this point is provided by her stance on the issue of love. There can be little doubt that she is understood by all to be on the side of the heroes who espouse the code of proper love; on occasion, other characters appeal to the nymphs to arbitrate conflicts of opinion in this area. Yet Galathée turns out to be one of the text's most flighty and flirtatious characters. Throughout she is intended to betroth Lindamor and she does give him concrete encouragement (see I, 363); but all the while she also welcomes the advances of the villain Polemas, seeks the love of Celadon, and finds herself irresistibly attracted to the knight Damon (III, 590 ff.). In this last case, the attraction is so strong that Galathée plans to hold Damon in reserve in the event that something should befall Lindamor. She thus betrays the heroic code of love with which, as a supposed champion of the heroic code, she is supposed to have identified.

At no point does the princess recognize the inconsistencies in her own character. But having betrayed the codes of love and of social hierarchy in the eyes of the reader, she shows her true nature to be at odds with the image that society has of her — or even the image she has of herself. This conflict goes far beyond the level of disguises which we have studied, for Galathée is scarcely involved in the overt game of disguise. These inconsistencies represent a mask which she wears within herself, deluding herself with regard to the duty imposed by her true nature, playing her own private game of deception as she confuses her identity beyond the point of clear recognition. In other words, she pretends within herself to be someone of whom less rigor is expected. The reader called upon to define Galathée's identity or true nature must look beyond the conflict of signs.

Astrée, the Woman Beloved

Many characters exhibit identifying signs which conflict with their true natures, or which contradict each other. Each of these situations signals a failure in the identifying process which makes it difficult for either characters or reader to recognize what someone really is. But of all the figures which appear in *L'Astrée*, none causes more confusion than the one for whom the work is named. Astrée, so easily identified on the surface, becomes a knot of contradictions when her character is examined in detail.

Outwardly she is one of the most clearly marked characters of the text. She is identified and recognized by her youth and her purportedly extraordinary beauty, her ancestry and her geographic origin, her social status (which, in fact, is as confused as that of all the other shepherds), and her personal past which is entered into the narrative; other stable markers include her handwriting and the fact that she is a storyteller. By these rather reliable signs, and by virtue of the fact that she represents the type of the woman beloved in the pastoral, the reader is able to fix Astrée as an easily recognizable figure. The most basic marker, her name, remains more or less constant as she does not seriously involve herself in the disguise game.

This name is, as noted before, that of the mythological goddess of justice. One would tend to see this association with justice as a marker of identity, but here the attributive process begins to falter. Astrée is both unjust and inconsistent — two qualities hardly suggested by her name. In fact, she is most unjust in her treatment of Celadon, and she is inconsistent in that she urges others (most notably Philis, I, 137) to be lenient in their treatment of the men who love them. Celadon is acutely aware of these facts as he asserts that Astrée's judgment is not like that of other people (II, 276).

Furthermore, one could take her outward appearance as the perfect shepherdess to be a sign pointing to the nature of the ideal woman. The indications she gives to society are those of a devoted, loving woman. But the identification process falters again as Astrée shows herself to be rather of an unpleasant nature: irascible and easily provoked, jealous, petty, and rash. These are scarcely the qualities one would expect of the archetypally desirable woman in the tradition of romance literature. Astrée, the woman beloved, turns out to be not entirely lovable.

Certain similarities with Galathée begin to emerge. Where Galathée seems at first glance to represent the ideal princess, Astrée stands ostensibly as the ideal shepherdess incorporating (or so we are told) all of the perfections of the shepherd society. Like Galathée, she is devoted on the surface to the principles which sustain her role. She too is identified by her commitment to a set of values — the bucolic ideals of courtesy, deference, tranquility, and love. Just as the circle of nymphs gravitates around Galathée and identifies with her, so the *bergères* gravitate about Astrée and refer themselves to her as they attempt to reflect the ideal. But as was the case for Galathée, there are also discrepencies in Astrée, between what she is taken to be and what she really is.

The most specific resemblance with Galathée lies in the fact that Astrée too offers arguments in defense of misalliance and thus stands, to some degree, in opposition to the tenets of social order on this issue. And just as in the case of Galathée, the argument in favor of misalliance is based not on actual inborn (though "disguised") nobility of the shepherds, but instead on a notion of the hierarchy of natural merit which, if it does not supersede the hierarchy of birth, at least supposedly parallels it in importance. The thought is phrased in the same terms as those we saw before, as Astrée says to Silvandre:

> Par vos merites... vous esgalez les perfections de Diane, et Diane par ses vertus surpasse la grandeur de Paris, et par ainsi l'inegalité n'est point telle qu'il faille par là accuser Amour d'aveuglement. (II, 203)

Another aspect of Astrée's identity which causes confusion is her sexuality. On the one hand, she is foremost known to reader and character alike as the incarnation of love, the beloved and loving heroine. It is she to whom the temple of love is dedicated (II, 176 ff.), and it is she for whom the entire, enormous tale of love is named. On the other hand, however, her sexual role is equivocal. We have mentioned the contacts with "Alexis" which, for Astrée, represent homosexual encounters (III, 598 and IV, 267). True, different levels of illusion are at work in these episodes, but Astrée does exceed the understood limits to the point where she hides in shame from an intruder.

More generally, the problem of sexual identity creates a crisis for the entire society of Forez, and Astrée's ambiguity serves well to exemplify it. Her affinity for members of her own sex, and her difficulty in relating to the man who loves her, illustrate internal conflicts within the ideal identity of the woman beloved. One might say that she finds it necessary to deprive her man of his manhood in order that he may approach her, for he may only approach her in the disguise of a woman. And when she says to "Alexis" that she could never love a man the way she loves "her" (IV, 263), the remark is not only ironic in the obvious way, based on the obvious disguise: Astrée in particular (like virtually all the characters) really relates more easily to members of her own sex because that relationship is not beset with the traps, illusions and misunderstandings of the heterogeneous relationship. Members of the same sex identify more readily with one another — even across lines of social status — because in such a relationship the obstacles and illusions that systematically impede heterosexual loves are not operative. Love is viewed as a conflict in which each sex regards the other as a potential enemy. Friendship among members of the same sex represents the only reliable kind of group solidarity.

As a consequence of these internal conflicts, Astrée appears at odds with herself. Both she and the reader cannot be sure of her true underlying nature and, as a result, she remains without a definitive identity, perhaps the most anomalous of the romance's characters in the reader's eyes. Her society does not experience doubts about her, but the reader does, and would be hard put to draw a coherent portrait of what she really is. Thus, she is always torn between her love for Celadon and the rigor which she insists upon, an ideal love who cannot be approached by the lover, for no clear reasons.

Celadon, the Lover

Celadon is another illustration of the problem of sexual identity in the society of *L'Astrée*. His crisis raises a paradox which is not unlike the ambiguities discovered in Galathée and Astrée. Celadon too stands ostensibly as a type, clearly defined by a system of outward identifying markers; closer scrutiny, nonetheless, reveals discrepancies between these outward signs and the true Celadon whom other, more subtle signs denote. In this, of course, he supplies a model for many of the text's major characters among whom the outward signs of identification conflict, as a rule, with deeper traits that are not immediately visible to fellow characters. But these traits do not escape the attentive reader.

Celadon's confusion is not particularly difficult to perceive. As the single character who embodies the perfect male lover in the shepherd society, Celadon obviously must be a paragon of masculinity. In certain ways he measures up to the role: with respect to the standards of the typical male identity code set out earlier, Celadon is strong, sensitive to the value systems of honor and love, faithful, impulsive yet obedient — in short, he displays all of the outward expected forms of conduct. Hence, and also in view of the reverential esteem in which Celadon is held by society and narrator alike, the reader's first and largely lasting impression is that Celadon is indeed the embodiment of the ideal masculine identity.

However, a more careful reader of *L'Astrée* soon enough realizes that in virtually all thematic aspects, the obvious first impression does not always prove to be reliable. Identity signs are often shown to be falsified by disguise, or unintentionally misleading. The sexual identity of Celadon is not exempt from this uncertainty. When discussing the notorious Celadon/Alexis transsexual disguise, we noted the underlying sexual ambiguity of the character; now we may explore the dynamics of this unique and very complex equivocal identification process.

That Celadon is not only symbolically but effectively emasculated throughout most of the text can scarcely be questioned since, as mentioned above, only as a woman may he approach his beloved. He also spends most of his narrative time disguised as a woman. In all, he dons three transsexual disguises and, together, they account for all of his presence in the text, with the exception of a few isolated scenes where he functions, and is recognized, as a man. In several instances, these scenes are passages of lament and soliloquy where Celadon steps out of his current transsexual disguise. What is more, after his attempted suicide on the fifth page of this *roman fleuve*, Celadon never again shows himself openly as a man to society; he is hidden in the Isoure palace by the nymphs, then conceals himself as a hermit, sneaking among the shepherds twice as a man, but only when they are asleep (II, 83 and II, 329 ff.). With the exception of these passages, society does not see Celadon as a male, indicating that his manhood is hidden not only by disguise, but also by his choice and actions. Indeed, one is tempted to conclude that he is not able to function in society as a man.

He seems predisposed to abdicate his masculinity, trading it for a false feminine identity on three different occasions. While he is thus prevented from pursuing his beloved under his own identity, he is paradoxically enabled to achieve at least one of the goals of love as set forth by Silvandre (I, 290 and II, 262): that the lover should die to himself and seek to "become" the beloved. While Celadon is disguised as Alexis, he does "become" a woman and does briefly exchange identities with Astrée (for example, III, 593). Celadon is acutely aware of the ramifications of this exchange, given the code of love which he espouses. He takes great delight in so "becoming" Astrée, even if the fuller realization of his love is precluded by the role which he is playing.

On the other hand, through the abdication of his male identity when donning the mask, Celadon reaches the point where his whole identity as a character is called into question, so profoundly does the disguising of the sexual role affect him. Indeed he accepts, and interacts with, the feminine identity so completely and so well that it begins to overtake him, forcing him to wonder:

> Mais quand je veux rentrer en moy-mesme, qui suis-je, qui redoute et qui desire? Suis-je Alexis? Non,... Suis-je Celadon? Non,... Je suis sans doute un meslange, et d'Alexis et de Celadon;... (IV, 252)

Certainly the mask is much more than physical: it becomes for Celadon an inner mask which finally hides his true identity even from himself. As a consequence, the identity change on the sexual level influences his entire being — physical and psychological — causing changes in conduct as well. Celadon adapts to the role physically and mentally. That he should act and appear as a woman is not surprising; neither is it surprising that he should change his voice to suit the part: in a text where Platonic values take precedence, and especially in a pastoral romance, the importance of the physical plane of existence (as well as its importance as a medium of communication) is secondary. But what does take the reader aback is the assumption of truly feminine characteristics by the disguised hero. For in this guise, he expresses ideas which are expected to be uniquely female: Alexis, for example, disparages the male sex for its customary inconstancy and egotistical intentions in love (III, 562), a complaint which is elsewhere reserved for women to make, the very sort of complaint by which he himself stands unjustly accused for the greater part of the text.

Now, given the nature of identity of the heroic couple — Astrée, who is taken to be the ideal woman beloved, and Celadon, who is taken to be the perfect lover — the reader takes note of indications that the heterosexual love relationship is necessarily beset with problems. Viewing the Astrée/Celadon relationship as an archetype in the text (an assumption not unwarranted since they are protagonists), one may state the problem in terms of the identification process. First the male lover is misjudged or misunderstood by the beloved, signaling an initial failure of the identification process whereby the man is not properly recognized by the woman; instead, she misconstrues his intentions (which, as a property of love, constitute a marker of identity), and consequently associates him with the antagonistic forces in the text. And naturally the question arises: how can characters identify one another if the heroic camp (those for truth, good, and purity of love) have recourse to the same devices as the antagonistic, corrupt forces? How can disguise and illusion serve the heroic code if that code is to remain consistent? The answer, of course, is that the heroic code is not consistent, and that the heroic code must remain an ideal abstraction in a less-than-perfect world.

Such a problem of identification hinders virtually every love relationship, and a second difficulty comes to the fore as a consequence. The lover is forced to alter his outward identity in order to resume his pursuit of the beloved. This produces the inevitable stalemate since, when the man finally reaches the beloved, he does so under an assumed identity (perhaps involving even a change of sexual identity), and thus is unable to see his love fulfilled. The process, lived by Celadon, turns into a pattern and occurs throughout the text.

Polemas, the Villain

No consideration of the overall identification process could be complete without the examination of the text's villains. Not only a sense of symmetry requires it, but also the circumstance that the very notion of a villain raises significant questions concerning the identification of characters. The case of Polemas, who is the principal antagonistic figure, will illustrate this point.

Polemas does not first appear to the reader as a villain. Quite to the contrary, he is introduced along with Silvandre very close to the beginning of the text (I, 31) at a time when the reader is aware that the principals are being presented in as quick and efficient a manner as possible. In this context of group introduction, Polemas first enters the text without any particularly distinctive characteristics. Illustrating a "figure du récit" that R. Debray-Genette has called anadiplosis,[1] Polemas progressively emerges from this quasi-anonymity to take

---

[1] Raymonde Debray-Genette, "Les figures du récit dans *Un coeur simple*," *Poétique* 3 (1970) 348-364.

the markers of the villain. It is interesting to observe that Polemas, and his antagonistic ally, Climante, are virtually the only characters of the text to be presented in this fashion: the others systematically appear with their outward signs clearly delineated by the narrator, or else (as more frequently occurs) with a story to tell which provides clear identifying markers for themselves and the characters in their intercalated narratives.

As the action unfolds, the villainy of Polemas increases until his plans for a political and military overthrow of Marcilly become manifest. By this point he has displayed all the markers of an archetypal villain: negative intent, sedition, lack of chivalry in combat, lack of deference to the object of his affections, etc. His status in the text is set squarely in opposition to the heroes, characterizing him as the central force pitted against the good and the social order.

This strong characterization, however, does not preclude certain inconsistencies in the identifying process — problems similar to those which were encountered in other major characters which we considered. Despite the fact that he is the principal negative character, Polemas too shows ambiguous signs which render his identification less clear than a simple typology of "villain" might indicate. First, Polemas is of most lofty birth: Leonide states that he is no less noble (in fact, possibly more noble) than Galathée (I 324); any villainy on his part thus mounts a tacit challenge to the facet of the social order known as the "code de noblesse," and calls into question any means of identification based on birth or "mérite."

But a difficulty arises in that Polemas sometimes shows sensitivity to that code of honor and protocol. In light of this, the society and even the narrator continue to treat Polemas with deference in spite of the knowledge of his evil propensities. And he does associate with heroes socially; his first appearance in the text is viewed through his reaction to Celadon's "suicide" "...dequoy Polemas fut marry, ayant tousjours aimé ceux de sa famille" (I, 31).

These confusing markers raise the question: what exactly is it that constitutes the identity of a villain in *L'Astrée*? This status cannot be simply attributed to those who victimize the innocent, since there are characters who do this without being otherwise marked as villainous. Tirinte, for example, abducts and almost kills the unwilling object of his love (IV, 128 ff.); yet he later accepts the consequences of his actions with remarkable grace and honor, and ends up a character of positive values (IV, 149-153). Nor can one point to the unchivalrous conduct of Polemas as the basic marker of his identity. Unchivalrous conduct is often exhibited by obviously positive characters. The latter sometimes set ambushes (as in IV, 743 ff.) or win combats by accident rather than skill. In fact, virtually all of the negative markers borne by Polemas are also borne by other positive or neutral characters to one degree or another, leaving the exact nature of villain-identification still uncertain.

The answer to the question lies probably in the observation that, in *L'Astrée*, the status of the villain, like that of the hero, is a relative notion, a matter of predisposition and general association in the final analysis. As the survey of the identification process has shown time after time, there are no absolutes in the text. No character is absolutely heroic, absolutely pure. Heroes sometimes do cowardly things: Ligdamon, for example, disguises as a woman to escape just prosecution for his actions. Heroes sometimes make ethical mistakes or get confused about the truth: witness the case of Galathée. Heroes make judgments according to double standards, as Adamas does on the issue of misalliance. And heroes deceive or are deceived by false appearances. Yet they remain unshakably rooted on the side of good in the reader's and the society's eyes.

Nor is the villain absolutely evil. He can be of very high birth, as are Polemas and all of the text's villainous kings. He can be just and display honorable conduct as, for example, king Gondebaut shows himself capable of doing. In that relative sense, the text is consistent, even if the characters are not. With regard to the process of identification there are no absolutes, either among the heroes or the villains.

Again ambivalence and lack of precision perturb the identifying process, and in this, d'Urfé represents something of a break with the classical pastoral tradition — a tradition of stock types. One strategy in *L'Astrée* which compensates the imprecision, but only for the reader, is the ready recourse to narratorial attribute. When the master narrator speaks of "la grande commodité que Polemas avoit eue de corrompre tous ceux qu'il avoit voulu attirer à sa faction" (IV, 565), he almost explicitly points to the evil nature of the character; for the rest, that is, for the society which does not enjoy the clarity of the narrator's discourse, identifying the villains remains difficult, and thus the villains are able to continue operating in society from positions of strength and respectability.

An identity marker which proves relatively reliable, and serves the reader and society alike, has to do with the character's political affiliation (caveat: there do exist spies, like Meronte, IV, 787, who purport to affiliate with the heroic camp). The point is that there is little in the makeup of the character (when considered in and of himself) that serves to typify him clearly and without qualification as a villain — or as a hero, for that matter. The whole issue of identification in this pastoral romance directs our attention to the fact that there are no unambiguous, static means of typification for characters. They may be grouped by various standards, but only in a general way. Examination in detail most often reveals idiosyncratic markers which can be confusing and ultimately paradoxical.

Hylas, the Character Apart

Hylas deserves special attention if only because he is most distinctive among characters in *L'Astrée*. In that sense he illustrates at its best the successful working of the principal function of the identification process: to distinguish one character from another. Hylas indeed stands out in bold relief among the overwhelming majority of flat characters in the text. Where others attract interest by their adherence to (and occasional departure from) the strict standards applied to pastoral characters, Hylas draws attention for a variety of reasons which come down to the fact that he is "different."

First and foremost, he steadfastly rebels against the society's dominant philosophy of love, doggedly arguing his beliefs and defending them against criticism from all quarters, before anyone who will listen.[2] No doubt, this opposition does not occur in a setting of true ideological debate, but Hylas' controversial opinions are nonetheless presented over and over with an almost cogent consistency. Furthermore, he maintains his principles nearly to the end of the text, where he is inevitably (and questionably) reintegrated into the pastoral code of love.[3]

We have already mentioned that Hylas is virtually the only character to be identified by hair color. The text insists many times that his hair is red; and this particular color, as opposed to fair or dark, has an additional distinctive connotation of being "apart" — here as well as in much of the tradition of literature, especially in the biblical tradition and in Spanish literature. Likewise, Hylas is one of a small group of young and eligible characters who are without a specific, great love. While even quite minor characters are identified by their love relationships, Hylas is not, and hence is "different."

---

[2] The figure of the cynical rebel is something of a *topos* in the romance tradition.
[3] This is the ending which Baro gives to the action. For our purposes, Hylas remains the renegade.

This startling uniqueness of Hylas may contribute to explaining why he is the major figure who is true to his markers of identity. Strangely enough indeed, it is Hylas, the great clown, who alone does not wear masks to deceive others or himself as to his identity, and manifests signs which are throughout consistent with what his true nature is perceived to be. His markers are manifold but trustworthy. With reference to love, he is the main apologist of inconstancy. Otherwise, he is the joker/trickster — the comedian who functions generally as an entertainer, showing the sense of humor for which he is reputed and considered attractive. He has a definite and complex past which he narrates into the record and which is consistent with his present; in fact, it serves partially to explain the present disposition of the character. The story of his past exemplifies his philosophy of love although, to be true, Hylas never carries it out fully in the present. In what could be construed as the only deviation from his identity markers, which markers would lead one to expect a great seducer, Hylas never actually seduces in the course of the action. Apart from the area of love, Hylas upholds the rest of the moral system: he espouses the heroic code of ethics and mounts no challenge to the heroes except in his philosophy of love. As a result, he remains a favorite of his fellow characters and reader alike; indeed, the reader may find him to be a refreshing variation of the customary pastoral figure.

No masking of his true nature occurs. Hylas knows what he is, he shows this nature overtly, and enables all others to recognize it without complication. In this respect also he stands quite alone: he is not given to illusion as are all other major characters. He thereby reinforces his uniqueness as a distinctive and remarkable figure whose process of identification is not encumbered with conflicting signs. No wonder that the feeble disguises which Hylas does attempt all fail and break down easily and quickly.

This ideal process of accurate identification with regard to the variable markers may also be observed with reference to Hylas' objective markers. He obviously stands apart by virtue of his name: he is the only major figure with the first initial "H," and while there are some few minor characters whose names begin with the letter, they also seem to stand apart for one reason or another. And again, he is the only character to be identified by a specific physical trait. His geographic origin is also unique: he comes from the island of Camargue, understood as an isolated spot, and no other character originates from there. The fact that he was born on an island sets him apart; Hylas himself underscores the uniqueness of his place of birth by describing it as "...destaché du reste de la terre" (I, 296), and hence apt to produce an "outlandish" character. One understands why Silvandre jokingly refers to Hylas' geographic origin as a possible explanation for the latter's aberrant beliefs (III, 359-360).

There is more: as regards ancestry and social status, Hylas is not one of the "noble" shepherds. Since he comes from Camargue, he cannot claim the knightly ancestry which, for other characters, survives under the clothes of Forez. Rather he must be a shepherd of shepherd stock, his forefathers having been admired for living "honnestement et selon leur condition" (I, 296). Thus his outward appearance relays accurate information about his essence. In addition, Hylas, more than others, relates details about his childhood and upbringing, to a degree which is quite rare in *L'Astrée*, and with an accuracy which is even rarer. Lastly, Hylas acquires distinction as a storyteller as well: his stories vary as he tells comical as well as serious tales; and he is an extremely effective storyteller, offering several narratives to his listeners.

In short, while other characters seem to find themselves hopelessly ensnared in the game of illusions and masks, Hylas emerges curiously as a figure of great sincerity. This distinction is in keeping with Hylas' singularity in many other areas; he has many qualities that render him unique, and the fact that he is true to his identity markers is only one more such quality. The important fact, however, is that thereby he demonstrates that identity in *L'Astrée* can be a direct process of signification after all, and hence that the undermining of the identities of other characters — Celadon, Astrée, Adamas, etc. — does not betoken an ideal process, but instead some form of subversion.

In most of these cases, identity (or the true nature of character) and markers of identity often appeared to oppose each other. Furthermore, characters often displayed contradictory markers, so that delineation of any true identity became a complicated or sometimes impossible task. No doubt, the characters in *L'Astrée* stand ostensibly as types which are easily delineated, and a cursory reading of the text does not undermine this typology. A more attentive examination, however, leads us to the awareness of subtle deviations from the general types, and of games involving identity in which the players themselves may be unaware of contradictions in their behavior.

As a group, the society in *L'Astrée* predicates its own order and its beliefs on the immutability of the order of the universe. Pronouncements to this effect abound: the natural world, the existence and intervention of the divine, and the society are all viewed ideologically as set along a great and unchanging chain of being. This philosophy is implicit in all the dicta of the text's metaphysicians and moralists, and is made explicit by Silvandre who describes the gradient of worth among beings, positing this scale as a reality of the natural order (I, 240-241). The society's entire philosophical system rests on this mechanical model of the universe, and as a result one would fully expect that the identity of character (ultimately a metaphysical phenomenon) be also set on this foundation, and hence, be a constant and discernable factor from start to finish. Yet we have seen that such is not the case, and we must try to account for this paradox.

The solution seems to be in the fact that, in this text as well as in many others, reality is not in line with, nor accountable to, philosophy. In this romance, the ideological foundation is undercut by the temporary absence of divine support. We are informed very early that the shepherds of Forez exchanged their nobility for protection from political worries, and that this exchange has been carried out through a covenant with the gods; yet the most general action related in the text centers on the political peril and invasion which Forez is constrained to suffer. Besides, as a further sign of isolation from the gods, the society is deprived of its mystical gauge of objective truth, the "fontaine de la Verité d'amour." Without both symbolic and concrete manifestations of truth, society is compelled to move and act in the domain of illusions. In an almost Derridian concept by which the sign (here, the marker of identity) is bereft of its guarantee of accurate correspondence between signifier and signified, communication is hindered because of the withdrawl of divine presence. With illusion dominating the communication processes, the society turns naturally to disguise as a way of solving identity problems, since disguise circumvents the awkward truth. Thus, in a world of illusion, society seeks to rectify its identification problems through the use of illusory identity. Other perturbances in the identification process may similarly be attributed to the general inconsistencies of a universe in semiotic disorder.

This survey has centered on the circumstances of these discrepancies, and served to assess the frequency with which they occur. We have seen the various ways in which so many of the romance's central figures deviate in their behavior from an identity so carefully established by means of markers. The pattern of deviation is so pronounced that any inquisitive reader, realizing the unreliability of narratorial associations, is often hard put to define a major character's identity with any concision. Some figures may be shown to exist mainly under a falsified identity: Astrée herself, like Celadon and many other shepherds, is actually of noble ancestry; Celadon spends most of his time in disguise and lives his existence through his mask and his interaction with it; Silvandre lives under an assumed name and condition which substitute for his true social status. And enough has been said about Galathée, Polemas and Adamas to obviate the need for further demonstration of the inconsistencies in their identification processes.

It has also been shown that identity is derived much less from individual characteristic traits than from markers related to function or association. One knows very little of Celadon as a character, for example, and he is typical of virtually every other figure in the text. We know little about his personality and even less about his physical aspect; he is instead identified by his value system and his love. Identification is carried out through the indirect process of association, superseding the direct means of identifying through characteristic trait of the individual.

We have also found two principal types of identity markers: those which are taken to be fixed and objective, and those which understood to be changeable and dependent upon the individual. The former set proved to be inconsistent and unreliable as indicators of the true identity or nature of a character. As may be expected, these direct means of identification are the ones to which the society first turns in order to define its members; but that same society has been seen as caught up in the game of illusion whereby disguises undermine the very markers of identification which are universally understood to be the most solid and the least likely to be challenged. Ultimately the variable and subjective markers proved to be more solidly based and of more significance; it is this set of indicators that the society and the reader find to be of more help because they involve behavior — an overt activity less susceptible to illusion — and because they involve functions which provide a great measure of a character's identity in a world of flat types. Nonetheless, one notices that all of the major markers of identification can be, and are, falsified as a matter of course.

The text thus sets up a very elaborate system of identification with both objective and subjective markers, only to undercut that system by rendering it unreliable. Characters introduce additional complexities into the system, either by displaying false signs pointing to natures other than their own, or by departing from the manner of conduct befitting a figure of their type. Characters who are marked to be pure, like Lycidas, are not; authoritative sources marked to be unimpeachable, like Adamas, may show flaws; female characters marked as sweet and lovable prove to be coy, implacable and exigent; male characters marked as being courageous, virile, and direct find it natural to disguise as women and spend their time in idle melancholy.

In short, there is, on the surface of *L'Astrée*, a carefully delineated system of markers, and below the surface there is a systematic departure from that delineation. Appearances, once again, do not denote reality, and the obvious and ostensible often must not be taken to be true. For the characters, life is seen through a "verre trompeur" (III, 568). For the reader who observes the characters, attempting to understand and categorize them, the same situation most often prevails.

Conclusion: The Society in Disguise

In chapter 7, we gave consideration to the question of markers of identity, recognized by society in the romance, and bearing on matters of social import. Family and ancestry are primary markers of an individual's recognized makeup, and they predetermine that character's social standing. Ostensibly the lines of separation between social classes are as fixed as a character's parentage; given the confusion which reigns in the area of identification in *L'Astrée*, society understandably counts on this degree of fixity for stability in the context in which all social dealings take place. In practical terms, characters low on the social ladder want to know before whom to bow, and nobles must have a clear idea of who their social inferiors are.

If our work has demonstrated anything, it has shown that the identification of the individual in *L'Astrée* is confusing at best: names are changed, faces (it seems) are rarely recognized after only the shortest separations, families are broken up, and of course, disguises flourish. Characters caught in a world where individuals can literally lose themselves, turn necessarily to the stability of the next highest human level for sense in the world: where the individual is quite often adrift without a clear understanding of his own identity or of the identity of others, perhaps the fixity of the social order will provide some clarity and make some sense in a turbulent world. And characters, from the top of the social ladder down to the bottom, do express their support and respect for the social order as it stands. Rare indeed, over the text's thousands of pages, are any characters' expressions of rebelliousness or insubordination in this regard; quite to the contrary, characters are almost uniformly interested in preserving the social status quo.

We observed that the marker of social status suffers nonetheless a degree of unreliability since it too can be subverted by misleading appearances. Status is understood to be the indicator of one's parentage, but when such is not the case, the appearances belie the inner reality for some specific reason, be it in the service of good or of evil. The marker of social position, one for which information is forthcoming in the narrative, is used for the purpose of classifying individuals; when appearances mislead, the social order itself is still intact and does not appear shaken by the error.

It remains for us to examine that social order, to see if it does indeed furnish the firm foundation for social dealings which is missing on the level of the individual. In spite of (and perhaps because of) society's inability to identify individuals reliably, that society — through its spokespersons — often reaffirms its own order and praises that order's stability. We must see if that praise is merited.

Now, for the reader who takes a sociocritical perspective on the text, these matters of social identity are crucial, but the interpretation of them must take into account the fact that the narrative constructs a fairy-tale world, far removed in time from seventeenth century France. Within the text itself, problems of social structure may not be immediately evident; furthermore, the same may be said for textual parallels with the social structure of France contemporary to the text's production. But since much of the action has to do with the preservation of social order, and many other markers of character identification are unstable, the system of social identification is of interest.

Our work on the subject of disguise has shown us that it has bewildering effects on characters and reader alike as they try to situate the individual in his or her place in society. To be sure, the tradition of Western literature offers many examples of nobility living in the guise of a lower social class: Daphnis and Chloe in the ancient Greek romance continue to spend the greater part of their time leading a pastoral life, even after having discovered their noble ancestry.[1] However, this issue does not cause a conflict of social identity in that tale. In *L'Astrée*, on the other hand, a similar situation is projected over the textual society to the point where the entire social stratification is undermined. And it is at this point where the reader may legitimately

---

[1] Longus, "Daphnis and Chloe," in *Three Greek Romances*, trans. Moses Hadas (Indianapolis, New York, Kansas City: Bobbs-Merrill, 1964) 68.

ask if this situation is not reflective of something in the society of d'Urfé's day.

Two specific problems come at once to the fore with regard to the fictional society within the text. They concern social status and they are suggested in both the (often done) study of the motif of love and the study of disguise and identity, related as the latter is to the *sémiologie du personnage* and hence to a collective semiology of the society. First is the issue of a disparity between the two types of aristocracy in the text: those who have retained their noble status, and those who choose to live as shepherds. We must ask ourselves to what end, and in what ways, the nobility is thus split and the ancestry of the shepherd class is being disguised. The other question involves the conspicuous absence of a discrete middle class. The other levels of the social ladder are amply represented, but no genuine "bourgeoisie" may be found in the society of *L'Astrée*. Even within the identification process whereby the society is seeking to define its own internal boundaries, no place is reserved for any bourgeoisie.

One answer may be proposed as a solution for both questions. It has already been observed that the text divides the existing nobility into two groups, thus creating an implicitly "better" shepherd class in Forez. Viewed in this light, the text may be seen as an attempt to engender a fictive "middle class" which would fill the gap traditionally existing between upper and lower classes in romance and other literatures. Into the void between the well-populated nobility and the peasant servant category, there falls this new social subdivision which the text postulates as the result of a pact with the gods, made for no apparent reason other than the desire to justify a pastoral setting — no apparent reason, that is, unless one is willing to attribute it to an experimentation with the social scheme. Let us explore this idea further.

The shepherd class, as it is represented in the Forez, inherits noble blood, and hence the instincts, virtue and prowess with which the nobility is endowed. This community of nobly born shepherds makes a collective choice to lead a life of simplicity and work (for example, each member has a flock of sheep to tend), yet all the while maintaining the characteristics of its inborn noble nature. In choosing this lifestyle, this subclass reunites three themes usually associated with the three social groups perceived as distinct entities in the seventeenth century: nobility (ancestry), middle-class (work), and peasantry (simplicity). On the other hand, the text does not treat these three factors as if they were equally important. Work in particular is discounted, and practically reduced to a subsidiary activity of the peasantry: shepherds tend their flocks without any profit motivation, are not seen in the act of buying or selling, in short are as dissimilar from bourgeois as they can be. Nor is the peasant-like simplicity stressed in any concrete way beyond or beneath a way of living that is, in general, leisurely. In that sense, the Forez shepherds, once the "tending of the flock" is disregarded (and indeed it can be disregarded as it does not create problems in the text), behave very much like the true nobles gathered at the Court, and whose leisure leaves them time and energy for either discourse and philosophy on love, or telling stories, or love, or political affairs. One could thus expect that the new "class," essentially a mirror-image of the old nobility, despite some distortions (if not corruptions), would be viewed as basically inferior to its model. In fact, however, the opposite relation prevails.

Indeed, a measure of doubt is cast upon the validity of the old nobility's lifestyle. Obligations, formalities, and protocol which beset them are sometimes described as boring and pointless, even by the nobles themselves. As a representative of the life of city and court, Circene is not alone when she says: "...je hay les contraintes, et les dissimulations des villes" (IV, 57). Other nobles take the occasion to speak out against the pomp and rigidity which characterize their lives. Leonide, for example, says of the shepherdesses :...je ne croy point qu'il y ait vie plus heureuse que la leur," after which it is said that "...elle resolut de changer les vanitez de la Cour à la simplicité de ceste vie" (I, 284). For that matter, virtually all outsiders, old-order nobles, for the most part, who come into contact with the shepherds remark that the latter are living the best of all possible existences. Throughout the entire work, it is not uncommon for visitors to express pleasant surprise at the degree of cultural sophistication which the shepherd society demonstrates. The reaction of the noble Leonide is quite typical, and she may be understood to speak for all those in the courtly society who are sympathetic to the shepherds' (heroic) code of values: "...je n'eusse pas pensé que les bergers de Lignon eussent esté si gentils ny si civilisez que je les trouvois,..." (II, 305).

Whenever their lifestyle is the object of praise, its most attractive element is its fusion of the nobility's culture and refinement with the ingenuousness and tranquility of a peasant condition. Viewed in this fashion the pastoral "disguise" which masks a noble caste takes on the positive aspect of striving for the perfect lifestyle, and the whole complicated concept of disguise is justified, even if it ends up causing confusion in social dealings.

Having modified the culture of the Court to suit their new situation, these nobles in shepherds' clothing control it and are acknowledged as the principal interpreters of culture: outsiders who dwell among the shepherds regularly adopt their ways and admire their particular refinement. Little fault can be found with their cultural directorship because their ancestral nobility and their natural superiority authorize and validate the modifications which they implement.

In creating this new social stratum, the shepherd class has also the explicit protection of the gods. This benevolent care is, of course, temporarily suspended in order to provide a test of the shepherd society's collective strength, but implicit divine support is scarcely in doubt at any point in the novel. Likewise the shepherds appear to have the blessing of other nobles in their effort to forge a new social position for themselves. Thus the text appears to go to great lengths to demonstrate that no code, either supernatural or social, is being transgressed by the artifice of a disguise which establishes a new "middle" group.

If the issue were to remain at this juncture, there would be no problem: one could simply assume that a harmonious society is re-formed as the new middle class and is absorbed into some preexisting social pattern. But difficulties arise when one searches for a satisfying explanation of this convenient process of reintegration and its relationship to the social reality of the times. These questions begin in fact to address the deeper meaning of the social scheme in *L'Astrée*.

The model of society in the extratextual world provides for a middle class which is identified in postfeudal times as the "bourgeoisie" and fills an area between aristocracy and peasantry. In the romance tradition prior to *L'Astrée*, the extratextual middle class is represented by merchants, craftsmen, money changers, etc., but is not identified as *bourgeoisie*. However, in the social structure which *L'Astrée* situates in Forez, the group which occupies this middle place is the noble shepherd community. Our hypothesis is that this special shepherd society is playing a role, wearing a lower-class disguise which ultimately proves to be problematic. In the first place, the members of this group are unable to escape completely the rigors of the code of nobility, despite their best efforts to withdraw from the court to the peaceful and secluded banks of the Lignon. They are afflicted (or blessed) with a hereditary sensitivity that is an integral part of the legacy inherited from past generations. This legacy makes up the inherent character of their segment of society, constituting the essence, the "être" which may be hidden, but never eradicated, under the outward clothing of shepherds. The disguise, in this instance, affects only the level of appearance, while the true underlying identity of nobility remains fundamentally unaltered — though masked nonetheless.

Consequently, a contradiction appears to occur between the two functions of the shepherd class: on the one hand, it seems to stand for the bourgeoisie since it is placed below the aristocracy in the text's social structure; on the other hand, it clearly forms an idealized nobility in its latent, true nature. How is this logical difference to be interpreted?

One possible explanation involves the omission of a properly bourgeois class from the text. The suppression of the bourgeoisie (and that of work) along with the withdrawal of the noble shepherds from society (and politics), may represent an unconscious reaction to the pressure which the middle class had been mounting upward against the nobility in the extratextual world at the time of the text's creation. This pressure originated, no doubt, in an economic expansion of activities carried out by the middle class but manifested itself and was perceived by society in two more visible areas: first, as the political promotion of bourgeois who, through various means, and sometimes by their merit, were elevated to the highest administrative positions in the kingdom, replacing the nobility in their traditional functions; and, in the second place, as the social promotion of the bourgeois who, through the purchase of letters of nobility, or through the procurement of offices which carried titles, or illegally, claimed to become nobles and to be entitled to the attendant privileges.

The results of this pressure are evident in the novel: there is uncertainty about what constitutes noble identity, and there is great semiotic confusion between appearances of identity and essence of character, between "être" and "paraître." In that perspective, the text may be seen to portray the working out of an extratextual social crisis through a subconscious reorganization of the novel's society. With the transformation of the noble shepherds into an apparent "middle" class, an unconscious desire is fulfilled: there is created a bourgeoisie which poses neither a challenge nor a threat to the nobility, contrary to the actual situation in the society of France in the seventeenth century. At the same time, a set of idealized "noble" values are projected upon that "good" bourgeoisie, displacing the real middle class values which posed a threat in the real world.

In order to complete this model of interpretation, there remains to determine in what disguised ways another place is found for the menacing values and activity which disturb the social order. The negative bourgeoisie of the real world, in the absence of a textual bourgeoisie with which it could identify, is indeed displaced into the "real" world within the text — the outside political force which threatens to disrupt the established system of Forez. Thus a fictional order is achieved by the suppression of the true bourgeoisie, on the one hand, and the nobility's withdrawal from the "real" society (the Court) to an ideal one (Forez), on the other hand; but then, the main sociopolitical conflict of the novel brings back disorder, as the intrusion of "reality" undermines the ideal dream. Violence, greed, and ambition do not remain suppressed by the artificial restructuring of the social code; these base attributes result in a threat to social order which the characters, under any guise, must confront.

Of course, there exists another possible model for the interpretation of the shepherd society in *L'Astrée*: it may in fact represent the bourgeoisie, not as it exists in the extratextual world, but rather as it should be ideally. According to this hypothesis, the noble shepherds are indeed the rising bourgeois who overtake and replace the nobility of the old order. But such an upheaval is not permissible by the established social standards (both in the text and in the real world). Hence, in *L'Astrée*, an unconscious (and contradictory) solution to the tension between reality and expectations justifies this rise of the bourgeoisie by ascribing to it many idealized characteristics of the nobility: lofty birth, though disguised, and all the virtues that go with it. And it is logical that there be no sign of the bourgeois values that are considered crass: the middle class here is idealized.

Because this new middle class is, by nature and by heredity, far from being mediocre or ordinary, one might well ask what it is that would bind it to its new status. How is the illusion carried off and made to appear genuine? These questions may be answered in two ways. First, the members of the new order are systematically made and shown to integrate with elements of the pastoral setting. While acknowledging their courtly ancestry, the text puts emphasis on all the ways in which they have truly become inhabitants of the countryside, very much attuned to nature and in harmony with their rustic environment. They ignore the usual pursuits of the nobility because they are taken with the life of doing what shepherds do.

The other means through which the survival of the new class is ensured rely on the concept of commitment: the Forez shepherds tend to display a marked degree of dedication to the principles upon which their new status is founded, in the way that Celadon, for example, makes it a point of honor to remain faithful to the ideals of his ancestors as he refuses the royal Galathée's promises of social advancement. When questioned by Adamas on this point, Celadon answers:

> ...toutes choses doivent se contenir dans les termes où la nature les a mises, et... comme il n'y a pas apparence qu'un rubis, pour beau et parfait qu'il soit, puisse devenir un diamant, celui aussi qui espere de s'eslever plus haut, ou pour mieux dire de changer de nature, et de se rendre autre chose que ce qu'il estoit, perd en vain et le temps et la peine. (I, 381)

Indeed it is the pact of the forefathers with the god which gives a status of divine mission to the foundation of the new social class. Celadon sees his place in society as allotted by nature; the covenant with the gods made in a past generation seems to afford divine permission for the formation of a new social stratum. One comes away with the impression that the shepherds' ancestors were commissioned by the gods to mold a discrete social unit to be placed between the aristocracy and the peasantry. Furthermore, it is noteworthy that, in light of the pronounced platonic content throughout d'Urfé's works, the new caste created here corresponds somewhat to the ideal middle class prescribed in Plato's *Republic*: the main druid, Adamas, is careful to point out that, even though Celadon is a shepherd, "il ne laissoit d'estre de l'ancien tige des chevaliers,..." (I, 368).

Through the sacred pact, then, the gods intend that the members of the new social unit bring with them from the old order all that is positive: valor, virtue, courtly sense of propriety, and leave behind all that is negative: pomp, rigidity, boring ritualism. There remains only for them to leave the Court and retreat to the Forez — that is, until they are needed as warriors (V, 9 ff.). That the shepherd society is committed to its station in life is evident, if only in the fact that its members are dedicated shepherds who care for their flocks (or so we are told) and are proud of their condition. But the issue of commitment goes beyond this point. In the course of the action of *L'Astrée*, the shepherds undergo a period of trial when the gods temporarily abandon them, failing to protect their society from invasion. Thus forced by the gods to sacrifice the peace of the pastoral life for a time, the shepherd society evolves to the point of making a commitment which is political in nature.

This evolution has three phases, not dissimilar to those traced for the motif of love in *L'Astrée* by Jacques Ehrmann.[2] First we encounter the society in its initial idyllic detachment, sheltered from the disturbances of the "outside" political world. The second phase is that of confusion and disorder as their region is violated by "foreign" invaders. This brings about the final stage, the synthesis of evolution seen in dialectical terms, whereby the shepherds decide to participate in the defense of the realm of their queen, Amasis. In making this choice they commit themselves to an active role in defending the social status quo, that is, the social order in which they constitute the ambiguous middle class.

The evolution of the shepherd class toward political commitment is paralleled by another development that is more personal in nature. The society is first seen enjoying freedom without responsibility. It subsequently passes through a crisis of consciousness and awakens to the task at hand. Finally, as the political threat is disposed of, the society witnesses the dawn of a new age of freedom, but with a new sense of responsibility and a new attitude of self-assurance and self-sufficiency. Thus, having first withdrawn from society in favor of "la vie champestre," the noble shepherds are eventually reintegrated into that society with a slightly enhanced social status. Even though they have sacrificed much with respect to rank, they reassume a crucial role as vital upholders of the social structure. They are productive in their work (we may assume) and in their efforts to defend the homeland; and they remain doubly committed to their new middle-class condition and to the perpetuation of the social and political order. Active and responsible (beginning with the ending parts of volume 4), they furnish that order with a firm basis of support — a point which buttresses the interpretation of the shepherd group as a "good" (that is, nonthreatening) and inspired bourgeoisie, an idealized class which shows no desire to upset the position of the aristocracy.

The shepherd class is understood to be descended from high nobility, with the result that both the upper and middle layers of society — the dominant groups — retain an aristocratic status in a moral sense. Were it not for one further detail, our study of the emergence of a new social stratum in *L'Astrée* would be complete at this point. But there is a lone character who stands apart from this system and is clearly distinguished as the one member of the new order who is

---

[2] Ehrmann 32.

not of lofty stock. This is, of course, Hylas — the black sheep, the renegade, the sole example of difference and deviance.

Hylas finds his identity in his very singularity, standing alone on virtually every issue except the central question of political affiliation. Whatever he is, he is no villain on that score; nonetheless he consistently establishes and reaffirms his individuality in the face of tradition, challenge, and even ridicule from all around him. The narrative sets him apart in every way. Different in beliefs as he is in physical appearance, Hylas is generally reputed for his propagation of a code of love which is diametrically opposed to the society's accepted standards of perpetual fidelity. At every turn his challenges and harangues are heard by his peers and, interestingly enough, he is never definitively argued down in logic. By the same token, however, he is never quite taken seriously, so that one may not really say that he represents a side in a general debate on love. On the contrary, as this author has tried elsewhere to show, the real discussion of codes of love takes place between Adamas and Silvandre.[3] So it is not the polemics of love which provide the basis for Hylas' singularity; this aspect of his character is only an outward sign, perhaps the most evident to society and reader alike, but with little substance beneath the surface.

The real basis of Hylas' distinctiveness is to be found instead in his social origins. All the quirks which he embodies are in keeping with the fact that his lineage is qualitatively different from that of the shepherds of Forez. He is the lone character of substance who hails from the true bourgeoisie. In this regard, as in most others, Hylas stands alone in the society of which he is, paradoxically, an important and popular member. No doubt, given his renegade character, his red hair, and all of the other traits which make him so different, it is only fitting that he be unique socially as well. This distinction, however, does not at all alienate him from the society; rather, it only underscores his peculiar and interesting status as the "harlequin," that folkloric figure who stands between two worlds without totally belonging to either. It is Hylas' nature to straddle two worlds: a foreigner to Forez, a challenge (yet not a threat) to certain social codes, and as we have seen, the character who stands as the original bourgeois in a new and emerging middle class. He represents the link which

---

[3] Gregorio, "Implications of the Love Debate."

is otherwise missing between upper and lower classes, the only genuine figure in a land of masks.

Hylas provides a trace of the true bourgeoisie in the novel. As a character, he bears the mark of the "expulsion" of the true middle class from the text in that he too is excluded from full participation in the society's activities. He is forced to stand at the door, as he does at Celadon's temple of love (II, 176 ff.), and looks at his world from a distance, as if from the outside. In short, he plays the role of the "trickster" — at once loved and cast out by the other members of his society. Strange as he may be, Hylas is thus the one major character of the text who is easily and consistently recognizable for what he is.

The rest of the characters of *L'Astrée* are left in a maze of illusions as they seek to identify each other. In a land where physical traits go unnoticed, where disguise reigns supreme, where even the distinction of gender identity becomes confused, it is perfectly consistent that there be confusion over distinctions of social class. Because many factors are at work in the process of establishing reliable codes of identity, the characters are forced to await the resolution of personal, political, and social crises before they arrive at an understanding of who they are and what they represent. What is certain is that love, far and away the dominant motif of action and discussion, must first reconcile itself with social codes: *mésalliance* will have to wait for another, more democratic day. In the meantime, the noble shepherds of Forez must continually try to clarify their social structure in order that their various conflicts find resolution.

D'Urfé's death left his masterwork well short of completion. There is no reason to assume, though, that these and the other conflicts we have discussed would have been brought to tidy conclusion. Our hindsight must not alter our critical vision: d'Urfé's time, like most times, was one of social change and development; what is more, d'Urfé's life and loves were, in similar fashion, not the stuff of boring tales. Antoine Adam phrases this very succinctly, saying of d'Urfé: "Si, quand il disserte, il est Sylvandre, il est, dans le courant de la vie, il est n'en doutons pas, le modèle de son charmant et volage Hylas."[4] If the text says one thing and demonstrates another, if characters profess one thing and do another, history shows that, in any event, the paradoxical nature of affairs is borne out in the author's life. Far from resolving the problems and inconsistencies in the text, at least these

[4] Adam 115.

considerations strike a chord in harmony with the text of the "despaired paradise," the forests of uncertainty in *L'Astrée*. If d'Urfé's masterwork does not answer the questions for us, we may find some solace in the fact that his life was consistent with his writings.

Appendix

Below is an alphabetized, annotated list of characters' names in *L'Astrée*, those who figure in the action narrated, and those who are mentioned in intercalated and inserted narratives. Included are all named characters, and those who pass only by some epithet or attributed sign (e.g." Le Maure"). Quotation marks are used to denote a name which is not a true one (e.g. "Alexis" is really Celadon in disguise). Some of the names are not of humans, such as Melampe (Astrée's dog) and Tautates (the divinity), but are included for the sake of completeness.

Adamas (chief druid; uncle of Leonide) name means "diamond" in Latin (III, 646)
Adelonde (wants to marry king Euric, III, 166)
Adraste (shepherd; love for Doris is unrequited, II, 342 ff.) goes mad when he loses Doris by Leonide's judgment (II, 379)
Aetius (popular Roman general, victim of schemes, character in digression on Roman history, II, 523 ff.)
Agis (becomes suitor of Leonide, I, 159 ff.)
Aglante (son of Arion who is friend of Menandre, loved by Silvanire)
Alaric (barbarian, II, 470) character in Adamas' inserted narrative
Alcandre (loves Circéne [Cyrcene])
Alcé (Astrée's father; had loved Amarillis and lost)
Alcidon (courtier; loves Daphnide; III, 52 ff.) dresses and plays at being a shepherd (III, 497)
Alcinie (mother of Dorinde)
Alcippe (father of Celadon)
Alciron (very mean, IV, 131 ff.; helps scheme of Tirinte)
Alcyre (knight; plays a ruse, III, 172 ff.)
Alderine (Bellimart's wife)
Alerante (Gondebaut's envoy, IV, 701)

"Alexis" (Celadon's disguise as Adamas' daughter)
Alindre (longtime servant of Asphale)
Amaranthe (daughter of Leon; friend of Bellinde)
Amarillis (Celadon's mother)
Amasis (queen of Marcilly; chief nymph) son is mentioned (I, 346)
Amasonte (aunt of Periandre, III, 360)
Amerine (woman for whom Lydias has killed a man) poisons self after Ligdamon does so; later, it is revealed that it was not poison (IV, 681)
Amidor (nephew of Phormion, intended by him for Diane, I, 198)
Amilcar (loves Palinice)
Aminthe (Celadon faked love for her, I, 18-19)
Amintor (knight; character in the ruse of Alcyre, III, 171 ff.)
Andrenic (and wife) old and trusted servants of Andrimarte
Andrimarte (lifelong friend of Childeric, falls for Silviane love requited in youth; Childeric becomes his rival) story (III, 649 ff.)
Androgene (shepherd; loves Dorisée, IV, 343)
Arcadius (son of Roman emperor, Theodose, II, 467) character in inserted narrative of Adamas
Archimbaut (powerful prince; causes uprising in Policandre's land, IV, 571 ff.) character in inserted narrative
Arcingentorix (father of Dorinde, IV, 163)
Ardilan (Gondebaut's servant and agent, IV, 364 ff.) makes advances to Darinée, Dorinde's servant, to further Gondebaut's advances to Dorinde; killed by Godomar (IV, 459-460)
Argantée (knight; nephew of Polemas, fights Damon, III, 289, dies in the fight)
Argire (queen of Pictes; arrives in Amasis' land, IV, 566)
Argonide (henchman of Polemas)
Arimant, [Arymant] (impoverished knight in Cisalpine Gaul, III, 365) enemy of governor Rhitimer; loves Cryseide
Arionte (son of Policandre, IV, 577) figures in inserted narrative
Aristandre (brother of Guyemants; had died for love of Silvie)
Aronte (killed by Lydias)
Asphale (brother of Filinte; his rival for Delphine, IV, 301)
Astrée
un astrologue (II, 557-558)
Ataulfe (succeeds Alaric, spares Rome; character in Adamas' inserted narrative, II, 467 ff.)
Attila (campaigns discussed, II, 523-524)
Avite (gouverneur of Godomar and Sigismond, IV, 369)
Aymée [Aimée] (Hylas' 3rd love, I, 305 ff.)
Azahyde (Suisse, son of Abariel; foster father of Silvandre) has daughter he intends for Silvandre in marriage

126 *The Pastoral Masquerade*

Belisard (offers to help Alcandre in his love for Circene, IV, 515 ff.)
Bellaris (servant & messenger of Arimant) disguises as Arimant to let Arimant escape captivity, on condition that he get Clarine as wife if he can get out III, 446)
Bellimart (enemy captain who aids Arimant, III, 437) also falls for Dorinde (IV, 166); previously married (to Alderine, IV, 194); dies (IV, 205)
Bellinde (sage; advises Silvandre, I, 281) wife of Celion, mother of Diane

Calidon (young shepherd; loves Celidée but loses out to older man) falls on side of imperfect love (III, 603-607)
Calirée (sister of Filandre; married without love to Gerestan) dies after hearing of Filandre's death (I, 309)
Carlis (loved Hylas, loved by Hermante who is Hylas' friend)
Celadon
Celidée (shepherdess, loved by older Thamire, II, 24 ff.) later disfigures self to test men's love (II, 444 ff.)
Celiodante (real son of Argire, IV, 573 ff.) renamed Kinicson; becomes Rosileon after loss of identity
"Celiodante" (substituted for the real Celiodante, IV, 576)
Cephise (Clorisene's daughter by previous marriage, IV, 578)
Ceraste (Servant & confidant of Sigismond, IV, 449)
Cerinte (brother of Palinice; loves Florice, IV, 498)
"Chevalier de Lindamor" sent by Lindamor to narrate story (III, 649 ff.) of Clidaman's death and Lindamor's wounding in the uprising against Childeric
Childeric (mentioned III, 588) genealogy (III, 650); son of Merovée; king of France; under his rule, court has become effeminate & soft (III, 651); people elect Gillon king out of disgust for Childeric
Clarine (Cryseide's confidante; daughter of her nurse)
Clarinte (wants to marry king Euric, III, 166)
Cleante (Celadon's guardian on trip, I, 120) (father of Aminthe)
"Cleomire" (name taken by Cryseide in disguise, III, 420)
Cleon (loves Tircis who loves her; dies of plague, I, 254)
Cleontine (woman; III, 297)
Clidaman (knight, loves Silvie); Polemas wants to profit by his absence (off to war) by marrying Galathée and becoming lord of province (III, 642); dies defending Childeric in popular uprising; remains loyal despite Childeric's difficult nature (III, 699)
Climante (fake druid); kills self (IV, 713)
Clindor
Clorange (intended to wed Cryseide by Rhitimer, III, 393)
Clorante (chief of Gondebaut's guard, IV, 440)
Clorian (brother of Palinice)

Cloridamante (druid, IV, 115)
Cloris (niece of Gerestan; Hylas' 5th love, I, 309); marries Rosidor (mutual love)
Clorisene (wife of Policandre; dies IV, 577)
Clotilde (woman; becomes close to Sigismond, IV, 354); pledges help in Sigismond's advances to Dorinde (IV, 409)
"Conseil des Six Cents": adjudicating body which gives poison to those seeking a just death
Corebe (rich shepherd, arranged in marriage to Astrée, I, 142)
Corilas (loves Stelle)
Crisante [Chrisante] (head druid, see II, 348-349)
Cryseide (Roman woman, prisoner)
Cyrcene [Circene] (shepherdess; Hylas' 6th love)

"la dame incognue" (conducts a secret love affair with Alcippe, I, 57-59)
Damon (knight, loves Madonte, II, 208 ff.); jumps headlong into river for love (II, 241); disguises as Chevalier du Tygre to save Madonte
Daphnide (woman at court; scorns love of Alcidon, III, 52); long story of how she loved Alcidon, (III, 81 ff.); dresses and plays at being a shepherdess (III, 497-498)
Daphnis (friend of Diane; loves Filandre)
Darinée (Dorinde's servant girl, IV, 364 ff.)
Delie (Daphnide's sister; go-between for Alcidon and Daphnide, III, 104-108)
Delphire (shepherdess)
Diamis (brother of Celion)
Diane (friend of Astrée: daughter of Celion and Bellinde); parents make pact with Phormion to wed offspring (I, 197)
Dorinde (shepherdess) spouts antimasculine remarks (IV, 109)
Doris (shepherdess, loved by Palemon and Adraste, II, 342 ff.)
Dorisée (loved by shepherd Androgene; friend of Eritrée)
"un druide" (character in Histoire de Damon, III, 302 ff.)

Egide (messenger; valet & friend of Ligdamon, I, 425)
Eleuman (mother of Tomantes)
Ergaste (awarded hand of Bellinde by her father) gives her up since she loves Celion
Ergaste (named after generous character above); son of Celion & Bellinde; is presumed dead in pillager raid, I, 419
Ericanthe (father of Tomantes)
Eritrée (friend of Dorisée; figures in story of Tomantes, IV, 307)
Eudoxe (woman loved by Ursace; has already died; II, 406 ff.); daughter of Placidie who is the daughter of Roman emperor named Theodose, II, 467 ff.; married to emperor Valentinian

Euphrosias (friend of Merindor)
Euric (succeeds Torrismond to throne; falls for Daphnide); rival of Alcidon for Daphnide (III, 81 ff.)

Filandre (brother of Calirée; loves Diane; dies, I, 232 ff.)
Filidas (daughter of Phormion, raised as a boy); falls for Filandre (I, 211); dies (I, 233)
Filinte (related to Tomantes; likes Delphine; IV, 297 ff.); brother of Asphale
Fleurial (old; acts as go-between for Galathée and Lindamor); bad memory for narration (II, 423-425)
Floriante (Hylas' 4th love, I, 308)
Florice (shepherdess; Hylas makes advances to her, II, 119); her parents appear (II, 159)
Fortune (shepherdess, chosen by Amour to teach Damon a lesson)
Fossinde (young girl chosen to narrate Silvanire's story)

Galathée (nymph, "la principale," daughter of Amasis)
Genseric (king of the Vandals, attacks Maxime at Eudoxe's behest, II, 545); character in digression on Roman history
Gillon (elected king by people disgusted with Childeric's effeminateness, III, 685-686)
Godomar (prince, son of Gondebaut, brother of Sigismond, IV, 369)
Gondebaut (king of the Bourguignons; takes Cryseide captive, III, 423, loves her); sees error of his ways and permits Cryseide to marry Arimant (III, 467)
Guyemants (rival of Clidaman for Silvie)

Halladin (squire of knight Damon)
Heracle (eunuch in inserted narrative of Valentinian, II, 519)
Hermante (Hylas' friend, I, 295 ff.)
Hipolyte (Astrée's mother)
Honorius (son of Roman emperor, Theodose, II, 467 ff.); character in Adamas' inserted narrative
Hylas

Kinicson (new name for the real Celiodante who is also Rosileon, IV, 635-642)

Laonice (shepherdess; loves Tyrcis)
Leon (friend of Bellinde's father, father of her friend, Amaranthe, I, 390)
Léonide (nymph)
Leontidas (wily executor of Madonte's father, II, 208 ff.); his wife remains suspicious of Damon's love for Madonte; see Leriane; plans to wed his nephew to Madonte

Leriane (girl, planted by Leontidas in retinue of Madonte); falls for Damon; seeks revenge for unrequited love, II, 219); has two cousins at court (II, 252) who are to defend her cause; jumps into fire out of guilt (II, 260)
Lerice (wife of Menandre)
Lerindas (sent by Galathée, III, 335 for information on Astrée et al.)
Ligdamon (knight, fond of Silvie) resembles Lydias exactly; poisons self after marrying Amerine (I, 434); reappears (IV, 678)
Ligonias (henchman of Polemas)
Lindamor (knight, loves Galathée)
Listandre (henchman of Polemas)
"Lucinde" (Celadon in disguise as a nymph, I, 456)
Lucindor (brother of Circene; loves Florice, IV, 496)
Lucine (midwife)
Lupeandre (in ruse, I, 141, accused of fathering Olimpe's baby)
Lycidas (brother of Celadon; loves Philis)
Lydias (exactly resembles Ligdamon, I, 429)
Lypandas [Lipandas] (friend of Aronte, wants to get even with Lydias)
Lysis (son of shepherd Genetian) loves Stelle

Madonthe (loved by Damon; is of higher class than the rival of Damon, Tersandre)
Malthée (shepherdess, finalist in beauty contest, I, 115); Alcippe wanted Celadon to marry her (I, 134)
Mandrague (magicienne)
Le Maure (kills Filidas, dies in fight with Filandre, I, 232)
Maxime (rich Roman; given Isidore in marriage by Valentinian, II, 514); gets self appointed emperor to succeed Valentinian whom he helped assassinate (II, 536-538)
Melampe (Astrée's dog)
Melandre (woman disguised as soldier, for whom Lydias has feigned love while they were in England, her homeland) goes by name of "Chevalier Triste"
Melusine (oracle-druide, female, figures in inserted narrative IV, 574)
Menandre (old shepherd; father of Silvanire, IV, 117 ff.) married to Lerice
mère de Cryseide (thwarts love of Cryseide Arimant, III, 393)
Méril (little page boy)
Merindor (suitor of Dorinde, IV, 162 ff.)
Meronte (bourgeois, loyal to Polemas, IV, 26)
Meroué, [Merovée] (leader of Ligdamon's army, I, 426; king and father of Childeric, III, 678, married to queen Methine)
Methine (wife of Merovée)
Mucutune (one of 3 daughters of king & queen of Vienne, IV, 353) sent to Vestals by Gondebaut who took Vienne

130 *The Pastoral Masquerade*

Olimbre (friend of Ursace, II, 406 ff.)
Olimpe (shepherdess with big ego, I, 134) gets pregnant by Lycidas (I, 135 ff.)
"Orithie" (Celadon's disguise as a shepherdess, I, 115)
Ormanthe (female, friend of Damon, II, 233, gets pregnant by Damon in complex love intrigue, II, 245 ff.)
Oronte (governor of Celiodante; preaches nobility, IV, 605 ff.)
Orsinde (daughter of Amasonte; befriends Cryseide, III, 360)

Palemon (jealous shepherd, loves Doris, II, 342 ff.) wins Doris by Leonide's judgment (II, 378)
Palinice (sister of Clorian) helped Hylas out of temple (see II, 111 ff.); loved by Amilcar
Pantesmon (friend of Doris' brother; likes Doris)
"Paris" (son of Adamas, cousin of Leonide)
Parthenopé (shepherdess)
Peledonte (henchman of Polemas)
père de Siline (counsels Aglante, IV, 121 ff.)
Periandre (Hylas' rival for Dorinde, II, 144)
Philis (Astrée's friend; loves Lycidas)
Phocion (Astrée's uncle; arranges marriage to Corebe) later wants to marry her off to Calidon (II, 433)
Pimandre (Amarillis' father, Celadon's grandfather, I, 49 ff.)
Polemas (villain; friend of Celadon's family, I, 31) loves Galathée; as noble or nobler than she (I, 324); develops mutual affection with Leonide (I, 371) which fades
Policandre (knight errant, becomes king, loves Argire, IV, 569 ff.)

Rosanire (princess; daughter of Policandre; traveling with Argire)
Rosidor (shepherd, loves & marries Cloris)
Rosileon (knight, gone mad, IV, 568 ff.) started out as slave, mutual love with Rosanire; saves king's life, wins freedom & knighthood
un Roy (who presides over the case of Madonte, II, 259)

Salian (brother of Stelle)
Semire (Corebe's servant; loves Astrée) had wronged her, but turns heroic in battle (IV, 801)
Sigeric (peaceful prince; becomes king; killed, II, 473) character in Adamas' inserted narrative
Sigismond (son of Gondebaut; widower of Amalberge, IV, 353) rival of his own father for Dorinde
Sileine (brother of Circene, IV, 536; used as pawn by Palinice to make others jealous, IV, 539 ff.); also brother of Lucindor

Siline (shepherdess destined by her father to Aglante)
Silvandre (loves Diane)
Silvanire (daughter of Menandre and Lerice; story, IV, 116 ff.)
Silviane (noble woman in court of Merovée; loved by Andrimarte)
Silvie (nymph)
Squilandre (Alcippe's forger, I, 142)
Stelle (shepherdess, inconstant, sister of Salian) her story (I, 181 ff.): she is capricious
Stilicon (II, 469 ff., seizes power in Rome, betrays the empire)
Stilliane [Stiliane] (one of Hylas' loves, I, 297)

Tamire (spars with Hylas on love, IV, 228 ff.)
Taramis (supernatural power whose oracle is consulted by Adamas, II, 312)
Taumantes (shepherd)
Tautates (the divinity worshipped by the druids)
Teombre (vain shepherd, II, 137)
Tersandre (Damon's rival for Madonte, II, 221 ff.) is of a lower class than Madonte, (II, 221 & II, 242); confused for Chevalier du Tygre (Damon); dies (III, 636-637)
Thamire (older man who loves young Celidée and wins, II, 24 ff.) his rival for her is his nephew, Calidon
Thrasile (head of Valentinian's guard, helps Maxime kill Valentinian and Heracle); character in digression on Roman history (II, 536 ff.)
Tirinte (considered a villain; loves Silvanire, IV, 127 ff.)
Tomantes (IV, 289, quibbles with Delphire); son of Ericanthe and Eleuman; mutual love with Delphire
Torrismond (king, succeeded by Euric, III, 81 ff.)
Tyrcis [Tircis] (laments dead beloved, Cleon)

Ursace (male; loves Eudoxe who has died; II, 406 ff.)

Valentinian (son of Placidie, intended by Theodose for Eudoxe) falls for Isidore (II, 492 ff.); succeeds Theodose as emperor
Verance (old man, cares for the real Celiodante, IV, 597)
vieil homme (avec petites filles) consulted by Dorinde (IV, 431-432)

Walia (elected king through Placidie's doing); character in Adamas' inserted narrative (II, 467 ff.)

Bibliography

Text

d'Urfé, Honoré. *L'Astrée*. Ed. H. Vaganay. Lyon: Masson, 1925-1928. 5 vols.

Works Consulted

Adam, Antoine. *Histoire de la littérature française au XVIIe siècle*. Vol. 1. Paris: Editions Domat Montchrestien, 1948. 5 vols. 1948-1956.
Alter, Jean V. "La Bande à Francion ou les pièges de l'histoire." *L'Esprit Créateur* 13.3 (Fall 1973) 183-195.
―――――. "Le Jeu des noms dans *Polexandre*." *Romanic Review* 67 (1976) 9-27.
―――――. "L'Etre et le paraître dans *Le Roman Comique*." *L'Esprit Créateur* 19.1 (Spring 1979) 3-13.
Bartsch, Karl, ed. *Chrestomathie de l'ancien français*. 12th ed. New York and London: Hafner, 1969.
Bochet, Henri. "*L'Astrée*: ses origines, son importance dans la formation de la littérature classique." Diss. Geneva, 1923.
Butler, Philip. "L'Erotisme dans *L'Astrée*." *Papers on French Seventeenth Century Literature* 10.2 (1978) 75-85.
Cali, Andrea and Carmela Ferrandes. "L'infrazione al codice: Il 'déguisement' nell'*Astrée* di Honoré d'Urfé." *Il romanzo al tempo di Luigi XIII*. Bari: Adriatica; Paris: Nizet, 1976. 13-38.
Campbell, Joseph. *The Masks of God: Occidental Mythology*. New York: Viking, 1976.
Carroll, Malcom G. "*L'Astrée*, or Virtue Corrupted." *Trivium* 8 (1973) 27-36.
Charron, Jean D. "Le Thème de la 'Métamorphose' dans *L'Astrée*." *XVIIe Siècle* 101 (4e trimestre 1973) 3-13.
Cherpack, Clifton. "Form and Ideas in *L'Astrée*." *Studies in Philology* 69.3 (July 1972) 320-333.

Chouinard, Daniel. "*L'Astrée* et la rhétorique: l'adaptation romanesque du genre judiciaire." *Papers on French Seventeenth Century Literature* 10.2 (1978) 41-56.

Cull, John T. "Androgyny in the Spanish Pastoral Novels." *Hispanic Review* 57 (1989) 317-334.

Debray-Genette, Raymonde. "Les Figures du récit dans *Un Coeur simple*." *Poétique* 3 (1970) 348-364.

DeLey, Herbert. "Two Modes of Thought in *L'Astrée*." *Yale French Studies* 49 (1973) 143-153.

Ehrmann, Jacques. *Un Paradis désespéré: l'amour et l'illusion dans* L'Astrée. New Haven: Yale University Press; Paris: Presses Universitaires de France, 1963.

Gaume, Maxime. "Magie et religion dans *L'Astrée*." *Revue d'Histoire Littéraire de la France* 77 (1977) 373-385.

Genette, Gérard. "Le Serpent dans la bergerie." *Figures I*. Paris: Editions du Seuil, 1966. 109-122.

Giorgi, Giorgetto. L'Astrée *di Honoré d'Urfé tra barocco e classicismo*. Florence: Nuova Italia, 1974.

Grange, André. "Le Langage des gestes et des attitudes dans la pastorale romanesque aux XVIe et XVIIe siècles." *Le Genre pastoral en Europe du XVe au XVIIe siècle*. Ed. Claude Longeon. Saint-Etienne: Publications de l'Université de Saint-Etienne, 1980. 183-191.

Gregorio, Laurence A. "The Character Under the Mask: Disguise and Identity in *L'Astrée*." Diss. University of Pennsylvania, 1980.

―――――. "Implications of the Love Debate in *L'Astrée*." *French Review* 56.1 (October 1982) 31-39.

Grieder, J. "Le Rôle de la religion dans la société de l'*Astrée*." *XVIIe Siècle* 93 (1972) 3-12.

Guichemerre, Roger. "Rois barbares et galants ('Histoire et romanesque dans quelques épisodes de *L'Astrée*')." *XVIIe Siècle* (1977) 43-68.

Hadas, Moses, trans. *Three Greek Romances*. Indianapolis, New York, Kansas City: Bobbs-Merrill, 1964.

Hamilton, Edith and Huntington Cairns, eds. *The Collected Dialogues of Plato*. New York: Bollingen Foundation, Pantheon Books, 1961.

Heiserman, Arthur. *The Novel before the Novel*. Chicago and London: University of Chicago Press, 1977.

Henein, Eglal. "Un Avatar de Clio." *Actes de Columbus*. Twenty-First Annual Conference of the North American Society for Seventeenth-Century French Literature, The Ohio State University, Columbus (April 6-8, 1989). Paris, Seattle and Tübingen: Biblio 17, Papers on French Seventeenth Century Literature, 1990.

―――――. "De l'Utilité de l'imposture: le statut des peintres dans *L'Astrée*." *Papers on French Seventeenth Century Literature* 16 (1989) 455-467.

———. "Les Vicissitudes de la quatrième partie de *L'Astrée*." *Revue d'Histoire Littéraire de la France* 6 (1990) 883-898.

Hersant, Yves. "Mythe et allégorie dans *L'Astrée*." *Mythe — Symbole — Roman*. Université de Picardie, Centre d'Etudes du Roman et du Romanesque; Actes du Colloque d'Amiens. Paris: Presses Universitaires de France, 1980. 29-46.

Highet, Gilbert. *The Classical Tradition*. New York and London: Oxford University Press, 1949.

Horowitz, Louise K. *Honoré d'Urfé*. Boston: Twayne, 1984.

———. "Where Have All the 'Old Knights' Gone? *L'Astrée*." *Romance: Generic Transformation from Chrétien de Troyes to Cervantes*. Ed. Kevin Brownlee. Hanover: University Press of New England for Dartmouth College, 1985.

Jehensen, Yvonne. "Realism in D'Urfé's *L'Astrée*." *Papers of French Seventeenth Century Literature* 10.2 (1978) 59-73.

Jones, R.O. *A Literary History of Spain: The Golden Age Prose and Poetry; The Sixteenth and Seventeenth Centuries*. London: Ernest Benn Ltd.; New York: Barnes and Noble, 1971.

Jourlait, Daniel. "La Mythologie dans *L'Astrée*." *L'Esprit Créateur* 16.2 (1976) 125-137.

Koch, Paule. "L'Ascèse du repos ou l'intention idéologique de *L'Astrée*." *Revue d'Histoire Littéraire de la France* 77 (1977) 386-398.

———. "Encore du nouveau sur *L'Astrée*." *Revue d'Histoire Littéraire de la France* 72 (1972) 385-399.

Magendie, Maurice. *Du Nouveau sur* L'Astrée. Paris: Champion, 1927.

———. L'Astrée: *analyse et extraits*. Paris: Perrin, 1928.

Morrissette, Bruce. "Structures de sensibilité baroque dans le roman préclassique." *Cahiers de l'Association Internationale des Etudes françaises* 11 (May 1959) 86-103.

Murnaghan, Sheila. *Disguise and Recognition in the* Odyssey. Princeton: Princeton University Press, 1987.

Nitze, William A. and E. Preston Dargan. *A History of French Literature*. 3rd ed. New York: Henry Holt, 1938.

Pollock, Mordeca Jane. "On Will and Reason in *L'Astrée*." *Kentucky Romance Quarterly* 28.3 (1981) 219-228.

Reure, O.-C. *La Vie et les oeuvres de Honoré d'Urfé*. Paris: Plon, 1910.

Rousset, J. *La Littérature de l'âge baroque en France*. Paris: Corti, 1953.

Sartre, Jean-Paul. *Qu'est-ce que la littérature?* Paris: Gallimard, 1948.

Sweetser, F.P., ed. *Les Cent Nouvelles Nouvelles*. Geneva and Paris: Droz, TLF, 1966.

Tilton, Elizabeth M. "Rhetorical Structures in the Silvanire Debate of *L'Astrée*." *Kentucky Romance Quarterly* 27 (1980) 299-311.

Virgil. *The Aeneid of Virgil*. Ed. T.E. Page. London: Macmillan, 1960.

Wine, Kathleen. "*L'Astrée*'s Landscapes and the Poetics of Baroque Fiction." *Symposium* 40.2 (1986) 141-153.

――――. "*L'Astrée*: Tomb or Fountain?" *L'Esprit Créateur* 25.1 (1985) 32-41.

Yon, Bernard. "Composition dans *L'Astrée*, composition de *L'Astrée*." *Papers on French Seventeenth Century Literature* 10.2 (1978) 9-27.

York, R.A. "Le Rhétorique dans *L'Astrée*." *XVIIe Siècle* 110-111 (1976) 13-24.

Zéraffa, Michel. "Raisons du coeur et raison de *L'Astrée*." *Le Récit amoureux*. Ed. and foreword Didier Coste; ed. Michel Zéraffa. Paris: Champ Vallon, 1984. 39-52.